P9-CDN-941

HELLAS

TRAVELS IN GREECE

HELLAS

TRAVELS IN GREECE

GEORG BRANDES

AUTHORIZED TRANSLATION
BY JACOB W. HARTMANN

ADELPHI COMPANY
NEW YORK

PRINTED IN THE UNITED STATES OF AMERICA

TRANSLATOR'S PREFACE

Georg Brandes has always been controversial; his essays and criticisms have hardly ever approached a subject, a movement, or a person, without having a definite desire to praise or condemn. His advocacy of *novorum hominum* has rarely been merely academic. And the man's entire career has in consequence been beset with hostilities of every kind, due in many cases to his emphatic espousal of such traits in his successive heroes as may not have received the general approbation.

No doubt Brandes has always leaned toward the classical element in civilization and more or less looked down upon the modern literature that is its offspring. Thus, when comparing Shakespeare's treatment of certain Greek characters in *Troilus and Cressida* with Homer's treatment of the same figures, Brandes finds himself impelled to declare:

"In the *Iliad,* these forms represent the outcome of the imagination of the noblest people of the

Mediterranean shores, unaffected by religious farces and alcohol; they are bright, glad, reverential fantasies, born in a warm sun under a deep blue sky. From Shakespeare they step forth travestied by the gloom and bitterness of a great poet of a northern race, of a stock civilized by Christianity, not by culture; a stock which, despite all the efforts of the Renaissance to give new birth to heathendom, has become, once for all, disciplined and habituated to look upon the senses as tempters which lead down into the mire; to which the pleasurable is the forbidden."

Brandes has long been a world figure, and his recent voluminous and scholarly tones on *Julius Cæsar, Michelangelo, Voltaire, Goethe,* and other great figures in world history have immediately found publishers in most of the civilized languages; not, of course, in English. A glance at these titles will show the present tendency of Brandes' studies, which has been noted by several writers: he is abandoning treatments of whole movements and trends, and limiting himself more and more to a discussion of the individual "great man," who now seems to sum up for him the greatest achievements of the race.

Brandes frequently quotes from the *Iliad* and the *Odyssey* in the present volume. He takes his quotations from the standard Danish translation. I have therefore felt justified in not attempting a new translation from the Greek, and have taken the appropriate passages from the standard English translations: that of Lan, Leaf, and Myers for the *Iliad,* and that of Butcher and Lang for the *Odyssey;* both were used as they appear in the Vincent Parke edition of *The Greek Classics* (New York, 1909).

JACOB WITTMER HARTMANN

New York, February 1, 1926

CONTENTS

HELLAS: TRAVELS IN GREECE

HOMER

HE who has beheld the tall isles of Greece has some idea of the nature of ancient Hellas. He breathes in its pure clean air, feels its sunlight, which burns and tans—burns mildly, tans pleasantly—walks through its groves of olive trees, drives beneath its palms, its cypresses, its fig trees with thick green figs, by paths bordered with hedges of hardy cactus.

If his meal consists of lamb roasted in olive oil, and his beverage is the good Greek country wine, it will appear to him that he is partaking of a Homeric repast.

He whose eyes have rested on the dark, slender men of modern Greece, and on their peasant girls, with their free, elastic tread, and on their little ones with their fiery black eyes—these children that still bear the names Aristidi and Aristoteli—has had a glimpse at the appearance of the ancient Greek country-dwellers.

For Homer has depicted conditions that remain the same forever. For example, in the Sixteenth Book of the *Iliad,* where he describes the little girl running after her mother:

"a fond little maid, that runs by her mother's side, and bids her mother take her up, snatching at her gown, and hinders her in her going, and tearfully looks at her."

Note also the comparison with Athena warning Menelaos against the arrows:

"even as a mother driveth a fly from her child that lieth in sweet slumber."

The Hellenic peasants remain to this day, as they were in antiquity, broad-shouldered, sober, hard-working, communicative.

For the most part, Hellas is a peninsula. The Peloponnesus is united with the Continent as a beech leaf is united with the trunk by its little stalk. But the country also includes islands, some of which extend along the western coast, while others are scattered between Greece and the coast of Asia Minor, seeming as close together as stones across a brook.

The fact that Hellas was cut up by mountain chains had the advantage of making it difficult to conquer the country, and furthermore of varying the character of the region, since the inhabitants of the various districts were pretty well isolated from each other, and each district was therefore able to develop its own peculiarities.

The country had been favorably treated by nature, for it was rich in sunlight and free from fogs, with the result that its people had no desire for artificial warmth or for many layers of heavy clothing.

Yet, it was not a luxuriant country; the soil was stony; and this again was a favorable endowment from nature, since it bestowed upon the inhabitants the frugality which serves as the germ of enterprise and aggressiveness. Herodotus says: "Poverty is our land's twin sister." Poverty was a spur to the application of energy, a defense against conquest, since the country held nothing that might serve as an allurement to the conqueror; finally, poverty was a powerful goad to pursue trade and invention, and to found colonies.

The climate neither enervated the Hellenes by excess of heat or unusually rich harvests, nor hardened and stiffened them by struggling with the cold and in the effort to attain warmth, food and clothing.

The distinguishing mark of Greece is not, however, alone in the fact that it is a mountainous southern country, but also in the fact of its long coast line. The sea, with its many bays and fjords, which indent the land, was a means of communication between the portions of the country that had been separated by the mountains. The sea had the effect of a great inland lake. It has often been observed that while the area of Hellas is smaller than that of Portugal, its coast line is longer than that of Spain.

Another characteristic trait of Greece is to be found in the fact that nothing appears of unnaturally large dimensions in this country. There are no extensive steppes or extensive wildernesses. The mountains are for the most part low, accessible, and rather to be considered as hills and ranges of hills. Mount Olympus, of course, was an exception.

The rivers are not broad or torrential; there are a number of streams and brooks. Springs are very frequent. The forests are not gigantic, but rather resemble large groves.

Thence, the Greek watchword: *Meden agan!*

Nothing must be too large! Everything within reasonable limits. *Moira* signifies not only Fate, but also the appropriate and reasonable measure of things.

The Greek—for natural reasons which are not far to seek—has an aversion for that which is strange, proportionless, formless in his eyes. What he loves and demands in nature and in man, as well as in art, is form. Roland slays one hundred thousand men with his sword; Homer reports no such incidents.

The Greek hates the infinite, which we barbarians deify under the name of the Endless, Eternity, that which embraces millions of years. Homer will not tolerate conceptions of infiniteness. That which is boundless, which has no ends, the Greek designates with the word *aperion,* which is also the word he uses for "silly nonsense."

We, with our official spirituality, live in the topmost story of a skyscraper. The Greek lived in a cabin with a garden, overlooking an arm of the sea.

Babylon had its huge structures; Egypt had its pyramids and sphynxes; Assyria and Persia had their gigantic monuments. In classic Greece, all things are relatively small.

When we find Ares, in Homer, covering several

acres (70,000 square feet), with his body when he falls, and emitting cries like the shouts of ten thousand warriors, we are dealing with a remnant of the primitive ages of the giants. Ordinarily, greatness in Hellas expresses itself in the correct interplay of parts; this greatness is an internal greatness.

In the Eleventh Book of the *Odyssey,* we read concerning the Cimmerians, a tribe living to the north of the Black Sea, and whose climate seems to have resembled that of Scotland or Denmark:

"Shrouded in mist and cloud, and never does the shining sun look down on them with his rays, neither when he climbs up the starry heavens, nor when again he turns earthward from the firmament, but deadly night is outspread over miserable mortals."

No country could have been less like Greece, which is both physically and spiritually the land of clarity and perspicacity.

Fogs produce extravagant reveries, maids of the mist, fairy children, the horses of Hel. Fogs encourage a preoccupation with the Beyond, with that which lies on the other side of the earth's atmosphere. But in this country, the sunlight afforded a sharp contrast of light and shade, therefore all art here has a plastic character and definite form; therefore, Greek ideas have a tendency to appear in relief.

In accord with this aversion to that which is infinite, religion, among the ancient Greeks, is the awe inherent in a relation with solemn things, not a feeling of the infinitude of the universe. The universe for the Greeks was the cosmos, order, beauty. Parallel with the Greek's passion for clearness, we find that religion is for him not the fear of a god who has issued commandments and prohibitions, but a feeling that is properly expressed in festive processions, songs, and dances.

No doubt the Greeks had a form of mysticism, both before and after the Homeric age. Even in the Homeric poems, as we have them, there are indications of the battles fought in the worship of Dionysus. And reference is twice made to the oracle at Delphi. But mysticism has been completely left behind in the epoch of these poems.

Beyond the gods lies Fate, whose immutability affords some similarity with inexorable death, or with the inescapable laws of nature, in our eyes.

The fact that Fate assumes the form of Nemesis is in accord with the fundamental feeling: nothing must be too large! There must be no arrogance!

No excess of self-esteem or ambition or exultation in strength! Praise is given to reasonable moderation, to harmony. The world for the Greek is not infinity, but a harmonious whole.

In the interior of the country, the Greek is, of course, a peasant. But his peculiar traits are best illustrated when he appears as a seaman, a pirate, a warrior, or a merchant. His character is best expressed when he rows or sails along the coasts in his boat. He goes ashore, asks questions, hears new and old gossip, tells a tale himself, is listened to, learns to avoid needless repetition, becomes skilled in omitting boring details, adds amusing adornments, condenses his wisdom of life in maxims. Having returned home, he reports and embellishes his adventures. He lies not a little, and is not free from poetic fabrication. He loves anecdotes; he even resolves his myths into anecdotes. These myths, which from the beginning were a reflection of nature, and a formulation of natural divinities, which were allegories or symbols, mysterious and significant, lose all their heaviness and mysticism under his treatment, and become—with few exceptions—fables to be told in a blithe and happy spirit. The symbol is relegated to the background. Plastic and picturesque beauty of presentation replaces that which is merely symbolical.

Verse takes its origin as a mnemonic device, centuries before the existence of artistic prose. It is difficult to memorize prose. Verse is associated with reminiscence, and the style is such as to permit of no reading between the lines, of no omissions.

When Odysseus says:

> "I will make trial of my father, whether he will know me again and be aware of me when he sees me,"

he adds another line, quite unnecessary to our modern way of thinking:

> "Or know me not, so long have I been away."

The Greek worship of the gods becomes a form of sacrifice in which the one who brings offering fully participates, but it also includes recitations, songs and dances, and has remained—like the myth—an entertaining recital.

He who produces the verses, as well as he who sings them, aims to entertain. The pious hearers receive a message of the joy of life and the joy of beauty.

When Herodotus tells us of the great religions

of the East, he really knows nothing about them. He considers the natural symbolical worship of the Assyrian Aphrodite, Mylitta, as an aberration, failing to understand that this voluptuous rite represents the creative fruitfulness of nature. He beholds in the numerous stones bearing carved figures of female genital organs, which Sesostris caused to be erected along the roads over which he passed as conqueror, symbols of the cowardice of the vanquished.

The Greek seaman was a pirate, or as we more elegantly put it, a Viking. A Viking expedition from Mycenæ to Western Asia was perhaps the cradle of the legends that we find worked over in the *Iliad*. The Greek seaman was also a colonizer. His colonies were not mere commercial factories like those of the Phœnicians before his day, and not mere instruments of exploitation, like those of the Romans after his time.

For centuries, the navigations of the colonizers, owing to the smallness of their boats, were limited to a cautious to and fro movement between the eastern coast of Greece and the western coast of Asia Minor.

But after the invention of the trireme, with its three banks of oarsmen, each higher than the other, and with the space it afforded for hundreds of additional persons, and its very much greater sea-worthiness than the ancient vessels, colonization proceeded by leaps and bounds.

Before 776 B.C., Æolian, Ionian, and Dorian colonies in Asia Minor had also colonized Thrace and the regions north of Bithynia. The city of Miletus alone, on the western coast of Asia, founded seventy-five or eighty cities.

Later, from 750 B.C. to 680 B.C., countless ships proceeded from the coast of Greece and Asia Minor, to Italy, Sicily, Northern Africa, Southern France. In the words of Cicero, a Greek crop was sown over all the lands of the barbarians.

The colonies were far more fruitful and therefore far more wealthy than Hellas itself. When the *Odyssey* depicts the splendor of the palace of Alcinous and Odysseus, the poet is transferring to the period of the Trojan wars his impressions from his own home among the coasts and isles of Asia Minor. These walls, tapestried with gold and silver, with bluish iron and molten glass, reveal an Asiatic imagination, concerned with things of splendor. The later, truly Greek architecture, is of an entirely different kind; like genuine Greek prose, it is a work of the *creative logic* of the

Greeks, which is their predominant characteristic.

The great poetry came from the colonies, from Chios, Lesbos, or Smyrna. For the colonies were superior to the metropolis in mental agility and mental freedom. The emigrants were young, able-bodied persons who were not petrified in their prejudices or bound down by traditions, like those who stayed at home. The colonial cities received Greeks of the most different tribes, who in Greece lived isolated; they mingled together and had constant instructive contact also with non-Greeks, and their *Wanderlust,* as well as their eagerness for knowledge, and the free play given to the imagination, were immensely stimulating. In one passage of the *Iliad,* we have an exceptional opportunity to peer into the mind of the poet, which otherwise is for the most part hidden from us.

"And even as when the mind of man darts speedily, of one that hath traveled over far lands, and considers in his wise heart, 'Would that I were here or there,' and he thinketh him of many things, so swiftly fled she in her eagerness, the lady Hera."

All efforts to restore the *Iliad* and the *Odyssey* in their original form have failed. We are dealing merely with two poorly restored masterpieces.

With the exception of persons who are naturally uncritical, there is probably not a man alive today who believes that a single poet named Homer wrote the *Iliad* and the *Odyssey,* not to mention the *Batrachomyomachia,* and the Homeric hymns, all of which are associated with the same great name.

I shall not touch here upon the thousand conjectures that have been made, but will merely present a short formulation of my own modest attempt at explanation; it is based on careful reflection, though not on an erudition comparable with that of Professor Gertz or Professor Heiberg.

It would be pure folly to assign to Homer all the works that pass under his name. The greatest philologist of antiquity, Aristophanes of Byzantium, and his world-famous disciple, Aristarchos of Samothrace, the greatest critic of ancient times, already expressed their sound judgments of this childish view.

As far as can be determined, the epic poetry of antiquity, at any rate, the *Iliad,* possibly also the *Odyssey,* originated on the island of Chios, near the coast of Asia. It is impossible to say whether the sublime poet who composed the First Book of the *Iliad* lived on this island or on Lesbos or in Smyrna.

For there are passages in which the poet who wrote the oldest, the only valuable portion of the Second Book of the *Iliad,* very distinctly depicts the specific region that lay before his eyes when he was a child or a youth. The warriors enter the land:

"And as the many tribes of feathered birds, wild geese or cranes or long-necked swans, on the Asian mead by Kaystrios' stream, fly hither and thither joying in their plumage, and with loud cries settle ever onwards, and the mead resounds; even so poured forth the many tribes of warriors from ships and huts into the Skamandrian plain."

The original poet, who was called Homer, because the poets of his school on Chios called themselves Homerides, may have been an Æolian who was brought up among Ionians. At any rate, we observe that the Æolians transformed the ancient legends into heroic epics, whereupon these epics, under the hands of the Ionians, were brought to their full beauty.

The founding of colonies began in 1034 B. C. The great Ionian national migration is assigned to the same year. The evolution of epic poetry may have set in immediately after this restless period. For my part, I am inclined to place the writing of the original *Iliad* at about 950 B. C., and that of the original *Odyssey* at about 850 B. C.

Since both the *Iliad* (IX, 380) and the *Odyssey* (IV, 125) express the greatest admiration of the Egyptian city of Thebes, which is declared then to have been at the height of its wealth and splendor, I cannot bring myself to assign dates that are fifty years later, as does Professor Heiberg, for by that time Thebes had already fallen from its glory.

In 943 B. C., Hector, King of Chios, a great-grandson of the founder of the kingdom, Amphiklos, ceased to govern the island. It seems reasonable to assume that the original Homer wished to preserve the memory of a prince of his home-land, by glorifying the name of Hector. And this would not be the only instance in which we are forced to conjecture that some attention was paid to existing conditions while the poems were being developed.

The attentive reader cannot fail to be struck by the fact that Nestor in the *Odyssey* suddenly is represented as having a son prominent in the *Odyssey,* whose name is Peisistratos, while in the *Iliad* the names of his sons are Antilochos and

Thrasymedes. The name seems to have been interpolated in Telemachia much later, as a mark of courtesy to the tyrant, perhaps three hundred years after the origin of the *Odyssey,* at the time when Peisistratos was causing a collection and editing of the Homeric poems to be made.

It appears beyond dispute to me that the original poets of the *Iliad* were of the Æolian tribe. The scene is Troy, which is on Æolian soil. The hero Achilles comes from Æolian Thessaly. Even if Agamemnon, the supreme king, is represented as king of Mycenæ in accordance with an old tradition, he is the ancestor of the kings in Æolian Kyme, and comes from the plains of Thessaly, and is called king of Argos, which means—according to Aristarchus himself—Thessaly. Since he comes from Thessaly, he chooses the nearby city of Aulis as a gathering place for the fleet, and makes ready to sacrifice his daughter there.

The poem does not originate in Mycenæ, for, in that city, the dead were *buried,* while in Homer they are *incinerated,* a procedure which naturally arose during the Ionian national migration. In Tiryns, implements of stone were used, while in Homer they are of copper or bronze.

The poems therefore originated in the period between the Mycenæan Era and the Classical Era.

The oldest sections of the poem, as may be clearly observed, have been altered from the Æolian form to an Ionian form. The older portions originated in Ionia, in the same dialect as the earlier portions, but with a more pronounced Ionian tinge. It does not seem entirely impossible to me that the action may originally have been assigned to Thessaly; in that case, it was a great national migration which created the legend of the military campaign overseas, and the Æolians do actually appear to have laid siege to Hissarlik, as the Trojan hill is now called.

These migrations forced warriors from the north way down into the Peloponnesus, wherefor we find Menelaus as king of Sparta, while a stream of Greeks, coming from the south, encountered in Asia another stream from Thessaly. This migration of nations, with its immediate concomitant of a flight of men, women and children, with a rapid construction of ships to facilitate the escape from the enemy on unknown waters and, therefore, with landings on foreign shores, where starvation and mass murder were expected to ensue, stirred the Greek spirit to its depths, filled it with valorous memories as well as with bitter experiences, and created Homer, *inasmuch* as it supplied the inner connection to a number of ballads that had hitherto been sung occasionally, molding them into a single epic. During this general flight by land and sea, the Ionian tribe became prominent, and the first fruits of its activities are what we are in the habit of calling the *Iliad* and the *Odyssey.*

At first glance we find quite a number of aids in a determination of the age of the poems: the burial of the dead is an older institution than the funeral pyre. Weapons of bronze are older than those of iron; the large leather shields, as tall as a man, are older than round shields of metal, and the shield in general older than the breastplate; locomotion by chariot, followed by hand to hand battle on foot, is older than action on horseback. And we usually find horse-riding mentioned in the Tenth Book of the *Iliad,* the so-called interpolated Doloneia, but not in the original Homer.

In general, it seems probable that the poet depicts the customs and conditions of his own time when he pretends to represent those of the past. Thus, the Bible has Moses, at the time of the Exodus from Egypt (Exodus xv) speak as if the promised land had already been conquered, while the narrator introduces his own knowledge concerning Edom, Moab, Canaan, even that concerning the dwelling of Jehovah, erected on Zion—lands and places that Moses never saw.—Yet, Homer frequently makes a definite effort to distinguish between past and present, to point out how much more powerful the men of the past were than those of his day, how much heavier the stones they could lift, etc.

The land of the Phæacians is a purified and beautified image of a new Ionian colony, free, proud, not obliged to enter into competition with any other people.

The Ionian tribe in the colonies of Western Asia was not so narrowly constricted and congested as were its rivals at home, the Lacedemonians. The folk genius of the Ionians was an animated communicative spirit, favoring change. The life of the Ionian was spent on the market place, in the popular assembly. When the *Odyssey* attempts to give some idea of the barbarism of the gigantic one-eyed Cyclopeans, the poet does not content himself with the mere statement that they neither plant nor sow. He says they have no popular assemblies, or, as we read in our translation of the poem:

"They have neither gatherings for council nor oracles of law."

On the other hand, smooth and swift though the course of Homer's language is, he has a keen sense for laconic qualities. He is describing the Spartan when he says, concerning Menelaus, king of Sparta, in the Third Book of the *Iliad*:

"Then Menelaus harangued fluently, in few words, but very clearly, seeing he was not long of speech, neither random."

But the contrasts between the Greek tribes among themselves do not prevent their standing as a compact mass, a sharply distinct race, as opposed to the Orient.

In the imagination of the Oriental, deluges, inundations, earthquakes, play a greater part than the delight in the beauty and qualities of nature. Never—as far as I know—does the Oriental make use of a single definite plant for purposes of comparison, as in the case when Odysseus says to Nausikaa:

"Great awe comes upon me as I look upon thee. Yet in Delos once I saw as goodly a thing; a young sapling of a palm tree springing by the altar of Apollo."

The Oriental is charmed with the regular recurrent life of nature wherever he thinks he has a glimpse of it, thus, with the superhuman majesty of the planetary system; and in his dances he attempts to represent the progress of the stars across the sky. The Greek never attempts any such thing; his dance was an expression of the joy of life, and we know the names of two hundred Greek dances.

The Hellene begins with a feeble attempt at personification; thus, Glaukos is the deep blue sea, while Athena is at first the pure azure of the sky. But the personification of nature becomes more and more outspoken. In the bends of the river, in the foamy outline of the waves, the Greek finds reflected the outlines of the female body, and he peoples the sea, the rivers, brooks and springs, with nymphs.

But then comes the time when these indefinite divine personalities, in the imagination of the Greek, are forced into the background in the presence of a new form: the hero. And the development of this new personality is a decisive event in the history of the Greek imagination.

In the Orient, where man was completely dazzled by the brilliancy of nature, there was only one hero; the despot, whose worshipers lay prostrate, in Assyria, as well as in Egypt and Persia. Israel did not tire of humbling itself before the supermundane power designated as the Lord. Nor did the Lord, on his part, ever tire of bidding, forbidding, chastising, punishing. And he who finds favor in the eyes of the Lord, namely, the Prophet, bids, forbids, chastises, and punishes in his name. In the Greek hero, man feels his own ability, his might, and sets himself up as a free beneficent power. At first, the hero is in many ways representative of physical strength alone; he is crude and cruel. But gradually he becomes more human and makes himself felt whenever a great task demands the putting forth of all his powers.

In Greece, each little district has its ancestors, who are handed down and worshiped: its celebrated benefactors, its heroes, whose honor may be maintained against the most glorious men of the neighboring states. The hero in this case is practically a demigod, but he remains none the less a citizen. He belongs to his race or to his city.

We can thus trace the process by which the *Iliad*

becomes gradually more and more extensive, by reason of the fact that each of the various regions wished to see its own hero distinguished before all others, wherefor we have, first Achilles, then Agamemnon, then Odysseus, Ajax, Diomedes, each having his day of glory, and even, in the Doloneia, the slain prince of the Thracians, celebrated for his wonderful horses and his never-seen weapons, which are so beautiful that they are hardly suited for mortal man. We also find emphasized the discipline and subordination prevailing in the camp of the Thracians. Even asleep, the soldiers lie on the ground in battle array.

Obviously, there was much commercial intercourse in the Homeric era between the Ionians and the Thracians. The Thracians sold the Ionians weapons and wine. In the *Iliad*—curiously enough—the Thracians are regarded as the peers of the Achæans. Later they were considered as a coarse, crude, almost ridiculous people. They seem to have passed through the same stages as the Irish and Flemings in modern history, and have also fallen from the estate of a once flourishing civilization.

Achilles offers, as a prize in the battle-games at the festival of Patroklos, a Thracian coat of armor, and a Thracian sword, these being more splendid than other weapons. In the *Iliad* (V, 462) Ares assumes the form of a Thracian leader. If he should have done this four hundred and fifty years later, in one of the comedies of Aristophanes, a spontaneous burst of laughter would have echoed over the theater.

It is a cup obtained by Priam from Thrace which is offered by him, toward the end of the *Iliad,* to Achilles in return for the body of Hector. This cup is Priam's most precious possession.

The Thracian wine is lauded as the best in existence; it is this wine that is served to Polyphemus by Odysseus, and it has such a delicious taste that Polyphemus becomes dead drunk with it, which is the occasion for his losing one of his eyes.—Evidently the poet is here dwelling on his own favorite wine. It should give cause for thought to observe that the only minstrel mentioned by name in the *Iliad* is a Thracian minstrel, Thamyris. The fact that he is blind in the poem, since the muses had deprived him of his sight as a punishment for his arrogance, was the point of departure for the legend that Homer himself was blind (*Iliad* II, 595–600). And this legend was naturally strengthened by the naïvely charming explanation in the so called Homeric Hymn—of much later date—to the Delphic Apollo:

> "And when a weary traveller demands,
> Who sings the sweetest on the Delian strands?
> Who strikes the most melodious lyre that rings
> At festal hour when minstrels touch the strings?
> Give ye this answer pleasing to my breast,
> The old blind man of Chios sings the best:
> With him compared all other lights are dim,
> None have surpassed and none shall equal him."

This prophecy did not fail to be justified by the event.

The first decisive trait in the spiritual history of Hellas was therefore its production of the hero.

The next decisive element is in the fact that the hero devours the gods by absorbing and including them.

The excavations undertaken within the past fifty years in Hissarlik, Mycenæ, on Cypress, on Crete, etc., have made us acquainted with the prehistoric, pre-Hellenic system of gods on the soil of Hellas. We find mystical symbols like the double hatchet, and the bull's horns, probably the same that were used on the Israelitic altar to symbolize the concentration of divine power.

Then follow, as we have already indicated, the rather faintly personified natural divinities. Zeus is originally the sky itself. Therefore, he is the gatherer of the clouds, therefore he descends in the form of rain, and casts the thunderbolts and rolls the thunder. The earth, or the goddess of Earth, is called in Homer now "she with the broad roads," now "the wide-breasted," and therefore also appears to assume human form. In Hesiod, the earth gives birth to the high hills and the deep-whirling Oceanus. We are still dealing here with nature-worship.

But when, in the *Iliad,* the beautifully flowing river of Xanthus becomes angry at Achilles because he has filled it with the corpses of the slain, and when it calls upon Hera for help, when faced with the fire of Hephaistus, we find the beginning of the process of transformation. When, in the Homeric Hymns to Aphrodite, the dryads take part, to be sure, in the round dance of the goddesses, but nevertheless live and die together with the great pines and oak-trees they inhabit, their divine character has been detached and liberated from nature.

Soon, the Greek nobility and the Greek petty kings, who were bursting with self-esteem, and who loved everything that was beautiful, began to worship the gods in their own form. The Olympus became a Greek family, presented a reflection of the splendor-loving and restlessly warlike life of the nobility. The gods pursue their personal inclinations in the most shameless manner. They are most faithful in their favor to him who is most generous in donations of fat gifts of cows and bulls as sacrificial offerings. They take it exceedingly ill, and treasure the evil memory, if anyone neglect to present them with the fine loin-cuts to which they are entitled. On the other hand, the gods and goddesses are firm friends to their faithful worshipers, and never fail to employ their (much limited) omnipotence and omnipresence to the advantage of these worshipers.

They are little disturbed by moral considerations. They bestow upon their favorites the ability to lie and deceive, and not only forgive them the crimes of theft and perjury, but even teach them to steal and perjure themselves, as Hermes in the Nineteenth Book of the *Odyssey* (verse 395), instructs Autolycus in these accomplishments. (In Shakespeare's *A Winter's Tale,* Autolycus has not yet forgotten these abilities.) Clever ruses amuse primitive tribes and are even esteemed by them, as Jacob's deception, practised with the cattle of Laban, is admired in the Bible, and as the Jutland peasant to this day admires him who is thoroughly capable of fleecing his victim in the sale of a horse.

The gods, in spite of the many moral maxims which were later interpolated in the poems, rarely give any thought to conceptions of right and wrong. They do not concern themselves with the good or evil of an action. They attach themselves with feminine affection to the individual, and whatever the individual does is right. Aphrodite could never even think of censuring Helen for having run off with Paris and deserted her husband. Athene would never even have thought of reminding Odysseus, who is so furious with his rivals, who consume his pigs and sheep, that he himself was a pirate for many years and made frequent marauding landings, stealing the property of others, slaying men, and selling women and children as slaves.

The gods are therefore attached, in the first place, to the person, later they become associated with the place where they are most zealously worshiped. Each of them is customarily named after such a locality.

We therefore do not find that the distinction between Greeks and Trojans amounts to a moral superiority of the latter over the former. The gods do not even imagine that one of the parties is better than the other. No doubt it was Paris's fault, in the period preceding the beginning of the poem, to have fallen in love with the fairest woman of earth; but it is only apparently for this reason that the conflict is being waged. The original motive has been lost, and there are as many gods in favor of Troy as in favor of the men of the Achæan fleet. If Troy is destroyed, it is not as a punishment, but because of a dictate of the only real power in existence, of Fate.

In prehistoric times, these gods overcame rude, colossal Giants and Titans. Now they are blessed.

On the earth below, life as a rule is passed as one passes a banquet, neither food, nor appetite, nor guests, nor diversions being absent. The life of the gods on Olympus is an eternal festive banquet in the open air. In the meantime they amuse themselves by observing or participating, as honored ancestors or gracious protectors, in the earthly struggles of their favorites, or in their difficult sea voyages.

There are times when things are rather gay on Mount Olympus. Zeus beats Hera within an inch of her life, or suspends her in the sky with a heavy ball attached to her feet, if she has irritated him more than usual. With the aid of Aphrodite's belt, she induces him one day to succumb to a very tender embrace, so that—after he has fallen asleep in her arms—she may bestow defeat upon his favorites, the Trojans. He then threatens her with a sound thrashing after awakening from his amorous intoxication.—In great rage, he casts out his son Hephaistus from Olympus on one occasion, with the result that the latter falls at full length upon the Island of Lemnos and never loses his limp thereafter. Here, as elsewhere, the humanizing of the natural gods has been carried out to fully human proportions.

In the case of Athene, we have the clearest instance of this transformation; Pallas is the daughter of Zeus, having sprung from his brow, the sunlit sky. She has no mother.

She is the clarity of the radiant atmosphere, its virgin whiteness, which charms and inspires with awe. About her, there is the invigorating briskness in the air that has been cleared by thunder and storm. Her eyes are of the blue of the sky. The eyes of the owl, which is her bird, see clearly in the dark.

Her violent birth has made her warlike, accoutered, formidable. Her birth to the accompaniment of thunder and lightning was not for no purpose. Never could the Hellene think of smiling about her as an old maid; she is Thought. Gradually she becomes also spirit and reason. She invents the arts; she tames the horse. It is she to whom the Athenians will later owe their active inventive spirit. Being Thought in motion, she has the majesty of the eternal.

A northern race, a nation with a cloudy sky, obtaining its religion from a German monk who imagined that in his apostasy he was approaching primitive Christianity, and who, moreover, fought with the Devil and the Pope, a northern race, nurtured by clericals, and accustomed to regard nature as accursed and the human race as inflicted with original sin, languishing for salvation—can hardly even imagine the frank enthusiasm with which the Athenian of ancient days intoned the hymn to Pallas Athene.

For him, she was high reason, radiant clarity, cleverness and wit, what we call genius, the providence and protectress of his city, young, pure, sound and strong.

Nevertheless, she was at the same time—in hoary

antiquity—extremely human. She has a pronounced affection for Achilles and makes an alliance with him against Hector.

Yet her affection for Odysseus is of another kind. It is her own character which she loves in Odysseus. She goes so far as almost to marvel at him. And wherefore? For his remarkable inventiveness in deception. The decisive passage is that in the *Odyssey* (XIII, 296), in which Odysseus has failed to recognize her when she has come to his assistance, first as a shepherd boy, and then as a robust woman, and he has filled her with lies untiringly. Suddenly she is struck by the similarity between the best head on earth and the best head on Olympus, which is herself. And she bursts out in the following terms of praise:

> "for that thou art of all men far the first in counsel and in discourse, and I in the company of all the gods win renown for my wit and wile. Yet thou knewest not me, Pallas Athene, daughter of Zeus."

Her divinity and humanity merge insensibly into each other. There is no sharper contrast than that between the relation here expressed and the relation of the Israelite to his law-giving God, or of the Christian to his judging divinity.

The primitive Greeks were life-loving, highly endowed children. Yet, their main trait is not their delight in life and lying, in the life of nature and the lies of necessity, that is expressed here, but in the fact that we find clearly illustrated the manner in which at first the heroic figure has here suggested the much tried, widely experienced man, who never loses sight of his object, and later the divine figure, characterized by insight and an all-embracing view, pure, radiant and warlike intelligence, merged together and become the central point in Greek life.

All things finally crystallize about the hero, either the brave and high-minded (like Achilles and Hector) or the inventive, cunning, hard-steeled (like Odysseus) : the hero attracts the gods to himself, remakes them in his image, and thus creates the graphic arts, sculpture, painting, as well as poetry.

The hero's fundamental trait is that of independence. In Homer, the hero does not fight in the ranks, but alone, in the chariot, or on foot. Neither among the Hellenes nor among the Trojans do we read of any kind of discipline. The poets have described their western Asiatic kinsmen, under the name of Achæans, and we find that among them independence is the source of a constantly renewed individuality. Never do we find a person in Homer who is completely subordinated to the idea of the state, as are the Spartans or Romans.

The hero dares, like Achilles, to blurt out harsh truths to his lord the king and to refuse to give him assistance. He fights even against gods, as Diomedes against Ares, and inflicts wounds upon the gods. The hero lives in a world that has not had much past history, and that has handed down but few depressing experiences. He is even less burdened with the prescriptions of a clearly formulated morality.

The ideal of the Ionian hero is that of sitting on one's throne as happy as a god, with the eagle, and of drinking life-giving wine in a richly embellished palace, at a groaning board, while a minstrel with his cithara or his lyre sings the hero's deeds.

The hero is not more than human. He may lose courage at times, though he be brave as a rule. The poet knows men and does not depict his heroes as did the Christian romanticists twenty-five centuries later.

Diomedes, otherwise quite courageous, is one day about to run away from battle, and Odysseus is obliged to call his attention to the shame that would ensue if Hector should get possession of their ships.

Even the bravest of the brave, Ajax, once loses courage and runs away.

In fact, Hector finally becomes so scared that he runs away, thrice making the circuit of Troy, and not stopping until Athene deceives him, in order to have him slain, by declaring that she is his brother coming to his assistance—whereupon she disappears—an action that would be considered quite shabby in the modern world.—Apollo also, on the other hand, behaves quite shabbily in his method of securing the slaying of Patroklos.

Homer knows mass enthusiasms no less than courage in the individual; but he also understands the phenomenon of panic. When the Atreid is pursuing in the *Iliad* (XI, 10), the Trojans flee post-haste over the plains before this single man, in order to find shelter behind the walls of the town.

The heroes of that far-off time did not strike attitudes; they remained men, they loved life and feared death. Not considering the world to be evil, and nature corrupt, the Hellene is fully assured of the fact that life is the source of all joys, and nature holy.

It follows that the Greek is not ashamed of his body, not even of the organs that do not serve the spirit. His comedians make merry with these organs without becoming obscene. And young girls marching in the religious procession bear at the head of the train, without embarrassment, the male symbol of fruitfulness.

The advantages of the Greek character lay in an equilibrium that has been abandoned by modern civilization. They never sacrificed this life for the hereafter; they never (except in the crude primitive days of human sacrifices) sacrificed man to divinity.

They did not feel man to be a mere nothing in the presence of divinity. They knew no dogmas, nor had they even—in Homer's day—any science to speak of.

Their advantage in those remote days was to have been the possessors for three thousand years of the most supple, strong, sound, beautiful bodies, fine senses, ready wit, a bright, proud spirit.

While the chief characteristic of Christianity is its preoccupation with death, the Greek regards the hereafter as a bleak land of shades; so we find it always described in Homer.

A single instance is to be found in the passage, probably a later interpolation, in which Proteus vows to Menelaus that he, who is related to Zeus himself through the person of Leda, his wife's mother, will not die in Argos, but will be led out to the limits of earth, to the Elysian fields, where life is blessed and where there is neither cold nor rain.

We may easily observe from the visit paid by Odysseus to the realm of the dead that Homer's imagination was a healthy imagination, with its home on earth, and that the Greeks much preferred life on earth to a life after death. Who can forget the wonderful words of Achilles to Odysseus:

"Nay, speak not comfortably to me of death, oh great Odysseus. Rather would I live on ground as the hireling of another, with a landless man who had no great livelihood, than bear sway among all the dead that be departed."

This canto surely was a portion of the oldest form of the *Odyssey*. How great a poet was the author of these lines! These words have been impressed in deathless characters on the minds of all reading and thinking persons throughout the world for nearly three thousand years, and there is no danger that they will be forgotten in the next three thousand years.

The Homeric poems, even when they depict the realm of the dead, are not figments of an overheated imagination, but of resplendent reason. Dante was, of course, a great poet, but his Hell is the product of a beadle's imagination and his Heaven is the vision of an enraptured dreamer. Nothing in the world could be less Greek than this emphasis of nightmare after nightmare, followed by a blind worship of a lady's smile.

The Hellene loves life, even though he be not afraid of that which follows it. The death of Socrates is depicted in Plato's *Phaido* without any sentimentality.

Homer's Greeks had the advantage over us of being much younger. In all their mental clarity and sobriety they had the seriousness and fire of youth, but also its enthusiasm and dash. They were not to create tragedy until four hundred years later. Homeric art compared with ours is like a wild flower compared with a cultivated plant, a babbling brook compared with a tinkling fountain.

The fact that desire is evil, and that nature itself induces us to commit sin, would have been an incomprehensible notion to Homer's Greeks. Never would they have thought of worshiping a god by fasting or by refraining from the drinking of wine, or by confessing their transgressions. They do not take crime lightly; but any crime may be expiated. And the Greeks worship the gods by adorning themselves in their finest raiment, and elevating themselves to the divine level to the best of their ability.

To be sure, in ancient days, when the mind was still crude, the gods were worshiped not with the blood of beasts but with the blood of men. In the myths we still find reminiscences of human sacrifices. Agamemnon's offering up of Iphigenia, for example, is somewhat parallel to the Old Testament story of the offering up of Jephtha's daughter, or of Abraham's offering up of Isaac; or in the New Testament, to the sacrifice of Jesus.

We have human sacrifices also in the *Iliad*. But it is important to point out the refinement of manners in the poet's day that is here displayed. Achilles offers up twelve Trojan youths on the grave of Patroklos. So ran the legend, such was the ancient custom. Obviously, the poet, in describing this solemn funeral, was obliged to present more than the sacrifice of sheep, oxen and dogs. But he is somewhat embarrassed and is obviously ashamed of this sacrifice of innocent prisoners. And although he frequently devotes a score of lines to depicting a banquet or a rare beaker, although he never neglects to describe the course of each thrust into the body of an opponent and the nature of each wound, the slaughter of the twelve aristocratic young men gets but a single line. First we are told that Achilles sacrificed two dogs. Then follows the statement:

"And twelve valiant sons of great-hearted Trojans he slew with the sword,"

Whereupon the poet adds:

"for he devised mischief in his heart."

This progressive refinement of manners, paralleled by an ennobling in the characters, may be traced in many passages in the Homeric poems.

Very probably the first story was to the effect that Achilles did not drag Hector's corpse attached to his chariot, but the living body of Hector. This would agree very well with his outburst:

"Would that my heart's desire could so bid me myself to carve and eat raw thy flesh, for the evil thou hast wrought me."

This mode of action on the part of Achilles is still recorded in Sophocles. Later he drags only the dead body. But even this procedure was much condemned by the Homeric poets. His action is called "shameful and shocking." The following disapproving words are also encountered:

"For Achilles had not a heart that was soft and easily touched, but his wrath was not difficult to arouse."

And yet, Achilles is one of the foremost heroes in the *Iliad*. During the many years, however, which elapsed before the *Iliad* and the *Odyssey* attained their final form, the view of life had changed somewhat. At a very late day we even find the interpolation of a conciliation between Achilles and Priam.

At first, women probably were the passive subjects of purchase, robbery and exchange. The wooer gave *hedna* for the bride. As is indicated by the use of the word *alfesiboia,* the woman's value was expressed in a number of cows; of course, money was unknown. It is a far cry from this condition to the refinement which we encounter in an Andromache, Helen, Nausikaa, or Penelope.

Originally, the divine couples, as well as the princely couples, were brother and sister. Later this condition is felt to be something not to be emphasized in those passages in the poems in which they embrace each other.

Thus, in the famous passage in the *Odyssey* in which Hephaistus, here represented as Aphrodite's husband (while in the *Iliad* he is married to one of the Graces), surprises and craftily captures the naked Ares and the naked Aphrodite in his ingenious net, upon his couch, we find not a word to indicate that they are brother and sister, as we also are not reminded of the fact that Hephaistus himself is Aphrodite's brother. But the man who wrote the Fifth Book of the *Iliad* had no need to be so delicate. There the offended Aphrodite states outright, as she throws herself down on her knees before her brother Ares, and begs him to lend her his horses:

> "Dear brother, save me and give me thy steeds."

Likewise, in the passage in the Fourth Book, when Hera, girded with the belt of Aphrodite, snatches up Zeus and is embraced by him in the golden cloud on Mount Ida, there is not a word to show that they are sister and brother.

On the contrary, in the Eighteenth Book, where the subject is not of erotic nature, but concerns merely a marital dispute, we find the following unembellished words:

"Meanwhile Zeus spake unto Hera his sister and wife."

In the same manner, the royal pair, Alcinous and Arete, were originally brother and sister, even in the *Eoioi,* according to Hesiod, but the passage was apparently altered at a later date, making the queen the daughter of a brother of the king. In the Seventh Book of the *Odyssey,* the passage begins with these words:

"Thou shalt find the queen first in the halls: Arete is the name whereby men call her, and she came even of those that begat the king Alcinous."

There follows, perhaps as a delicate tribute to the views of propriety of a later day, a long explanation to the effect that Arete is only the daughter of a brother of Alcinous.

A similar very instructive expression of the increasing delicacy of feeling is found in the fact that the oldest vase paintings representing the naked Odysseus as a ship-wrecked man facing Nausikaa, depict him as extending a conciliatory olive branch toward her, but it is well known that Homer puts the matter as follows:

"Therewith the goodly Odysseus crept out from under the coppice, having broken with his strong hand a leafy bough from the thick wood, to hold athwart his body, that it might hide his nakedness withal."

Child-like as the poet none the less is, he not only delights in every beautiful object in nature, but particularly in every example of artificial imitation, especially in life-like counterfeits, such as that of the golden dogs before the palace of Alcinous, who know nothing of age or death, or in the automatons in human form, constructed by Hephaistus, on which Hephaistus supports himself as he walks.

Homer knows no real sculpture, but only metal work embossed and chiseled like the shield of Achilles. Casting in molds was not invented until three hundred years later, in 640 B. C. He knows nothing of work in marble, as he knows nothing of money or written characters.

Values were not measured in money but in oxen.

When Glaukos and Diomedes learn, in the heat of battle, that their fathers were guest-friends to each other, and when these two adversaries thereupon exchange their armor, we read:

"But now Zeus son of Kronos took from Glaukos his wits, in that he made exchange with Diomedes Tydeus' son of golden armor for bronze, the price of five score oxen for the price of nine."

Writing was obviously as little known as money. To be sure, we have found remnants of picture-writing and character-writing on the island of Crete, dating from the pre-Hellenic period, and the Phœnician writing is also quite old. But the personages of Homer know no writing. The only passage in which anything resembling writing is mentioned is found in the much (and later) patched Sixth Book of the *Iliad* where Proitus tries to have Bellerophon slain by handing him a sad piece of news:

"graving in a folded tablet many deadly things, and bade him show these to Anteia's father, that he might be slain."

It could hardly have been a letter, and besides, the passage may have been inserted at a later date.

Perhaps one might mention the passage, in the

Seventh Book of the *Iliad,* in which the chieftains cast lots to determine which of them shall fight the duel with Hector. Nestor shakes the dice in his helmet. One die falls out of the helmet. The herald immediately brings this die to the kings of the Achæans, but none of them knows this token; all shake their heads:

"But when he came, bearing it everywhither through the throng, to him that had marked it and cast it in the helm, even glorious Aias, then he held forth his hand, and the herald stood by him and put it therein. And Aias saw and knew the token on the lot, and rejoiced in heart."

There is nothing to indicate that this symbol was a letter of the alphabet.

We cannot, of course, infer that the poet was not himself able to write because he does not speak of writing. Virgil does not mention writing either.

Homer repeatedly mentions the broiling of meat on a spit, never speaks of boiled meat; for in the passage in the *Iliad* (XXI, 362) in which the river Xanthus boils when Hephaistus torments it with his fire, the river is being compared with a caldron that seethes with the boiling of pig's fat. Fish are never mentioned in the Homeric poems as an article of food, yet there are two references in the *Odyssey* (IV, 368, and XII, 251) to fisheries. In the former passage, Odysseus's followers on the Island of Pharos, near Egypt, are induced by hunger to fish "with bent hooks," while we read in the second passage the following figurative narration:

"Even as when a fisher on some headland lets down with a long rod his baits for a snare to the little fishes below, casting into the deep the horn of an ox of the homestead, and as he catches each flings it writhing ashore, so writhing were they borne upward to the cliff."

We may infer that fish was despised as a food stuff, not being considered a proper food for a warrior. Perhaps oysters were more popular. At any rate, the *Iliad* describes oyster-fishing in much detail (XVI, 747).

While we may therefore not definitely infer anything from the fact that the poems themselves do not mention writing, we find that they were left to the mercies of oral tradition for centuries, since memories were then strong, and we know that the Greek alphabet was not finally completed until half a thousand years later, namely, in 403 B.C. And even when not a few were already able to read, preference was probably given to a recitation of the poems, with musical accompaniment, rather than to a reading of them in private.

Dispassionate though the epic mode of presentation may be, we nevertheless find a passion for the art of poetry breaking forth at times. Flaubert saw in all the events of life illusions destined to serve as objects for description. Homer already had this feeling.

Alcinous asks Odysseus not to shed tears for the destruction of the Greeks and Trojans:

> "All this the gods have fashioned, and have woven the skein of death for man, that there might be a song in the ears even of the folk of after-time."

It is reasonable to ask what were the qualities and abilities with which the Homeric poets approached their task of representation.

In the first place, we may mention the uniformity of their culture, the clarity and transparence of their language. They were so fortunate as to possess a language without words borrowed from foreign languages, and which therefore was understood by all. Their civilization was original, while ours is a patchwork. A scientific monograph written in a modern language is a hodgepodge of the vulgate tongue, embellished with corrupt Greek and medieval Latin. Furthermore, their art was the product of a uniform civilization, while even the most splendid of the modern arts have declined to be a mere *mixtum compositum*. Michelangelo shapes a Christ who looks like a Jupiter; Correggio's angels are like little pages undressed; Shakespeare's Romeo is at bottom an Englishman; Goethe creates a Ferrara which is more like Weimar; Racine produces an Achilles wearing a Seventeenth Century wig.

In the most ancient Greek art, we already find that uniformity of structure which is a condition for true civilization.

In the first place, these poets have a sober gift of observation, an acute sense of reality. Homer has all the knowledge of his time, being thoroughly acquainted with the working of the soil, the chase, the art of the armorer, navigation, weaving, the construction of houses, strategy and tactics, medicine. We even find mention in the *Iliad* of a female physician (XI, 740), the blonde Agamede:

"And she knew all the drugs that the wide earth nourished."

It is characteristic of the high civilization in the *Iliad* that we do not find a single treatment of wounds by means of magic incantations. Arrows or darts are drawn out, the flow of blood is stopped, salves are applied, the pain of the victim is appeased with wine or with mixed beverages. There is no trace of superstitious practises. So far had enlightenment advanced among the circles of the nobility. In the *Odyssey,* which was more popular in its origin (XIX, 457), there is but one passage presenting a trace of such superstition. Here a charm is spoken (ἐπαοιδῇ) in order to stay the black blood ("with a song of healing").

The vision of these poets, and the great extent of their familiarity with every phenomenon in nature, with the sky, the earth, and the sea, with the entire animal kingdom, with all the vicissitudes of the chase and warfare, are revealed in the celebrated Homeric figures of speech, which are very numerous, particularly in the *Iliad,* and which are always developed into complete miniatures, while the element of similarity is relegated entirely to the background, sometimes almost forgotten, in the poet's delight in the process of detailed description. The poets of the *Iliad* see far more clearly than they think. In the *Odyssey,* comparisons are far more impressive, but relatively few in number.

An example of a figure of the first kind is the following, from the *Iliad:*

"Even as the harvesters, advancing to meet each other over a rich man's land, lay low the grain in their course, either the wheat or the barley, while sheaf falls after sheaf, even so the Achaians and Trojans rushed forth to encounter each other."

The image of the action of the harvester is carried out with care and objectiveness, but the comparison is not a striking one.

Quite different is the effect of the figure in which the ship-wrecked Odysseus is represented as hiding for the night under a pile of leaves:

"And as when a man hath hidden away a brand in the black embers at an upland farm, one that hath no neighbors nigh, and so saveth the seed of fire, that he may not have to seek a light otherwhere, even so did Odysseus cover him with the leaves."

At times, comparisons are so awkward as to appear comical in our eyes. For instance, we read in the *Odyssey* (XV, 175):

"Even as yonder eagle came down from the hill, the place of his birth and kin, and snatched away the goose that was fostered in the house, even so shall Odysseus return home after much trial and long wanderings and take vengeance."

In one place, the poet with his sharp gift of observation, which regards none of the things as ridiculous that may appear ridiculous to us, unites in a description of the same man a comparison with the lion and a comparison with the ass.

Ajax is compared with a lion by reason of his strength, with an ass by reason of his obstinacy. It is well known that Holberg, governed by the taste of the Eighteenth Century, considered this combination grotesque (in *Peder Paars*[1]) and writes the following lines of parody in the Third Canto of the First Book:

"Quite like an ass standing in a fruitful field."

In Homer the passage reads:

"And as when hounds and country folk drive a tawny lion from the mid-fold of the kine, and suffer him not to carry away the fattest of the herd; all night they watch, and he in great desire for the flesh maketh his onset, but takes nothing thereby, for thick the darts fly from strong hands against him, and burning brands, and these he

[1] A mock heroic poem in iambs (1719–1720, by the Dano-Norwegian poet Ludwig Holberg (1684–1754).—TRANSLATOR.

dreads for all his fury, and in the dawn he departeth with vexed heart."

Thereupon follows, without any transition:

"And as when a lazy ass going past a field hath the better of the boys with him, an ass that hath had many a cudgel broken about his sides, and he fareth into the deep crop, and wasteth it, while the boys smite him with cudgels, and feeble is the force of them, but yet with might and main they drive him forth, when he hath had his fill of fodder, even so did the high-hearted Trojans and allies, called from many lands, smite great Aias, son of Telamon, with darts on the center of his shield."

The gift of observation in the Homeric poems is combined with an absolutely surprising ability to create individual persons.

In the *Iliad* alone, among the women, we have the clearly defined pictures of Andromache, Hekuba and Helen, and among the men, there are splendid objective pictures of Achilles, Hector, Paris, Odysseus, Thersites, and the three brilliantly outlined old men, Nestor, Phoinix, Priam.

Less consistent, in the various books of the *Iliad,* is the figure of Agamemnon. In the First and

Eleventh he is manly, though unjust and tyrannical; in the Second, Ninth, and Fourteenth, he seems devoid of character. No clearly defined physiognomy may be attached to Ajax or Diomedes.

Very few figures run through both poems. We have only Nestor, Odysseus, Menelaus, and Helen, who is the only woman represented in both the *Iliad* and the *Odyssey*. She is the object of the authors' most delicate and affectionate treatment. As no thought was further from the Greeks than to imagine that there could be anything comical about Menelaus in his capacity as a deceived husband, so we also find that nothing derogatory is spoken of Helen, in either poem, except by herself, although it is she who is to blame for all the trials of the Greeks and for all the misfortunes of the Trojans. She is the object of an unfaltering respect and admiration, being ennobled by her extraordinary beauty.

The action of the *Iliad* occupies barely five days; that of the *Odyssey* about thirty. The *Iliad* contains more than fifteen thousand verses, the *Odyssey* more than twelve thousand. With its many interpolations, the *Iliad* is rather extensive, and yet, it is quite short as compared with the Oriental epics; the *Mahabharata,* the ancient Indian epic, has one hundred thousand couplets.

There are detached sections in the *Iliad,* like the passage containing the list of ships, which are not in their proper places. The description of the shield of Achilles is also an interpolation, drawn with great care, with a delight in nature and in art. In order to afford an occasion for this description, one of the poets was obliged to have Achilles lose the shield, in other words, lend Patroklos his arms, a childish and awkward notion. Patroklos, thus accoutered, is to frighten the Trojans. But Homer constantly emphasizes the closeness with which the cuirass fits the fighter's body. Now Achilles is of gigantic stature; how can his armor fit Patroklos? And Achilles does not state that he recognizes his weapons on Hector's body, which would surely have doubled his rage. Patroklos's borrowing of the weapons is in reality of no significance. It is the subject of a silly masquerade. Patroklos is a deciding element in the conflict because he leads fresh troops to battle, not because he is in disguise, an incident which is introduced merely in order to produce an occasion for inserting a description of the new shield forged by Hephaistus for Achilles.

When I was a young man, and anyone requested me to read aloud something of recent interest, I used to enjoy reading—as a joke—the Ninth Book of the *Iliad,* the message to Achilles, which I love and esteem. I was then of the opinion that this book was a portion of the oldest section of the *Iliad.* I am no longer of that opinion. The fact that this book was added later is clearly apparent if only from the situation that Achilles is there promised everything which he later, in the Eleventh Book, desires to obtain from Agamemnon, and hopes to get from him in the Sixteenth Book (XI, 609, and XVI, 35). In other words, Achilles, in these books, is unaware of the fact that he has already definitely rejected the offer of the Atreid.

The Ninth Book presents instructive prospects. Behind the poem concerning the rage of Achilles we glimpse an older, perhaps symbolical, poem on the rage of Meleager.

The fact that the aged Phoinix did not originally participate in this mission is revealed in the no less than six passages (verses 182, 183, 192, 196, 197, 198), in which the dual form is retained instead of the plural, although there are three messengers.

But who would like to dispense with the character of Phoinix, who was the first tutor of Achilles, and who speaks the charming verses:

"Yea, I reared thee to this greatness, thou godlike Achilles, with my heart's love; for with none other wouldst thou go into the feast, neither take meat in the hall, till that I had set thee upon my knees and stayed thee with the savory morsel cut first for thee, and put the wine-cup to thy lips. Oft hast thou stained the doublet on my breast with sputtering of wine in thy sorry helplessness."

Even Achilles nowhere describes himself in prouder words than in this passage:

"Neither have I any profit for that I endured tribulation of soul, even staking my life in fight. Even as a hen bringeth her unfledged chickens each morsel as she winneth it, and with herself it goeth hard, even so I was wont to watch out many a sleepless night and pass through many bloody days of battle, warring with folk for their women's sake. Twelve cities of men have I laid waste from ship-board, and from land eleven, I do you to wit, throughout deep-soiled Troy-land; out of all these took I many goodly treasures and would bring and give them all to Agamemnon son of Atreus, and he staying behind amid the fleet ships would take them and portion out some few but keep the most. Now some he gave to be meeds of honor to the princes and the kings, and theirs are left untouched; only from me among all the Achaians took he my darling lady and keepeth her—let him sleep beside her and take his joy! But why must the Argives make war on the Trojans? why hath Atreides gathered his hosts and led them hither? is it not for lovely-haired Helen's sake? Do then the sons of Atreus alone of mortal men love their wives? surely whatsoever man is good and sound of mind loveth his own and cherisheth her, even as I too loved mine with all my heart, though but the captive of my spear."

The famous illustration of the poet's powers of characterization is the celebrated parting scene between Andromache and Hector. It is in the Sixth Book of the *Iliad,* having been obviously put in the wrong place in the final arrangement. It should be at the beginning of the Twenty-second Book, in which Hector is slain.

The entire Sixth Book, in spite of many beautiful portions, is merely a piece of patchwork. It is in this book that we suddenly find a temple to Athene, with a seated statue of the goddess, in the castle of Ilion, a temple mentioned nowhere else by either the *Iliad* or the *Odyssey,* which speak only of altars. In the *Odyssey,* Athene helps to get the wooden horse up the mound of Ilion, but no temple is mentioned. The temple is a later addition.

But what a breach this makes in the lovely scene in which little Astyanax, in the arms of his nurse, is frightened by the plumes of Hector's helmet and must put the helmet down on the ground! And how dreadful is an interruption, introduced by the improper placing of the scene, into Andromache's eternal words:

"Nay, Hector, thou art to me father and lady mother, yea and brother, even as thou art my goodly husband. Come now, have pity and abide here upon the tower."

The faithful description of the details of Andromache's fears for her son, after the death of Hector, is very impressive:

"Now thou to the house of Hades beneath the secret places of the earth departest, and me in bitter mourning thou leavest a widow in thy halls: and thy son is but an infant child—son of unhappy parents, thee and me—nor shalt thou profit him, Hector, since thou art dead, neither he thee. . . . For other men shall seize his lands. The day of orphanage sundereth a child from his fellows, and his head is bowed down ever, and his cheeks are wet with tears. And in his need the child seeketh his father's friends, plucking this one by cloak and that by coat and one of them that pity him holdeth his cup a little to his mouth, and moisteneth his lips, but his palate he moisteneth not. And some child unorphaned thrusteth him from the feast with blows and taunting words, 'Out with thee! no father of thine is at our board.' Then weeping to his widowed mother shall he return, even Astyanax, who erst upon his father's knee ate only marrow and fat flesh of sheep."

He who has read *The Trojan Women,* by Euripides, knows how much worse the boy's lot actually was. The mother is obliged to yield him up to be slain, and is herself made a slave-woman, taken by force by the son of Achilles. The great tragic poets intensified the dark and gloomy elements in the Homeric materials.

In Homer, experience is that of an intelligent child, the mode of expression is that of primitive man, the mode of feeling is simply human. We are made to sympathize with the embittered Achilles, with the fleeing Hector, with the irregularities of Helen, and yet do not lose sight of our ideals of courage, mercy, chastity without prudery. The poets seem to have the gift of sympathizing with both sides. For that reason, the Greeks, four centuries later, became the creators of the tragedy.

The most richly gifted nation of antiquity is a thing of the past. The intelligent race that now bears its name still preserves a number of its qualities, but they are not the best and greatest traits of its long artistic supremacy.

Since the Renaissance, however, there has existed in Europe a thinly scattered group of men who have been imbued with the Hellenic spirit, who have been attracted to plastic and lucid thinking, who have been hostile to vague and illogical conceptions, to formless and infinite things, who have valued joy and fair visions, who have had no use for asceticism for its own sake, but only as a means to an end.

These men have called the general attention to the Greek spirit, to Greek greatness, to Greek freedom of thought, mindless of the fact that this earned for them the epithets of godless and frivolous men, or any other characterization that might have entered the minds of the mob in the course of centuries.

One of these men, quite unlearned when compared with the great philologists, now stands before the latter, and on the fiftieth anniversary of his first public expression of opinion in Denmark, thanks them for their kind attention, and hopes that as a speaker he has not always thrashed the empty air, and that as a writer he has not always written on the sand.

THE ODYSSEY

IT is of the greatest interest as an aid to an understanding of the manner in which the poems came to be, of the life and activities of a poet in the Homeric period, about 800 or 900 B. C., to read what is recorded on this subject in the Homeric poems themselves.

In the *Iliad,* the older of the two, we find very little concerning verse and minstrelsy. There is a passage in the Ninth Book, the passage in which the messengers arrive at the tent of Achilles and take him by surprise:

"So they came to the huts and ships of the Myrmidons, and found their king taking his pleasure of a loud lyre, fair, of curious work, with a silver cross-bar upon it. . . . Therein he was delighting his soul, and singing the glories of heroes."

We also find a cursory reference to the Thracian poet, Thamyris, also the wedding hymn and the festive hymn at Linos in the Eighteenth Book, and finally, the minstrels' song as a part of the funeral of Hector:

"And the others when they had brought him to the famous house, laid him on a fretted bed, and set beside him minstrels leaders of the dirge, who wailed a mournful lay, while the women made moan with them."

That is all we find in the *Iliad* concerning poetry. The *Odyssey* is far more detailed in its treatment of poetry.

In the very first book of the *Odyssey,* we find a herald mentioned as handing the beauteous lyre to the minstrel Phemios, who is forced to sing for the suitors at one of their banquets in the house of Odysseus, and we read, at the very outset, that

"the wooers minded them of other things, even of the song and dance: for these are the crown of the feast."

Phemios sings, and the subject of his song, which seizes Penelope and torments her, is quite calculated to surprise modern readers:

"And his song was of the pitiful return of the Achæans, that Pallas Athene laid on them as they returned from Troy."

These verses afford us a glimpse of an entirely different legend than that upon which the main content of our *Odyssey* is built up; for, in all the rest of the *Odyssey,* as well as in the *Iliad,* Athene is entirely in favor of the Achæans, and is particularly the protectress of Odysseus.

But Athene was originally his worst enemy, as is confirmed in the outright statement of Hermes to the goddess Calypso, spoken in a situation where there could be no intention on the part of one divinity to deceive the other. Hermes states that Zeus has made up his mind: Calypso, after living together with Odysseus for seven years, must now desert him. Zeus knows that a man is living in Calypso's cave, more wretched than any other among those who fought before Ilion. In the tenth year, they

"sacked the city and departed homeward. Yet on the way they sinned against Athene, and she raised upon them an evil blast and long waves of the sea. Then all the rest of his good company was lost."

When Penelope, depressed by the tale of the tribulations of the Achæans, doubly disturbing to her in her sad widow's estate, begs the minstrel to break off this song and substitute for it one of the many popular ballads he knows about the gods and heroes, her young son defends the poet and at the same time gives us some information concerning the nature of the demands then made of a minstrel:

"As for him it is no blame if he sings the ill-faring of the Danæns; for men always prize that song the most, which rings newest in their ears."

People, therefore, had no great liking for the old stories.

The *Odyssey,* among other things, aims to represent the calling of the poet as sublime, and the poet himself as inspired. The poets of this epic take no pains to beat about the bush in speaking in their own interest on many occasions.

When Odysseus, at the end of the poem, is inclined to slay Phemios with all the others who have given any assistance to his wife's impudent wooers, or who have participated in their banquets and revelries, Phemios steps forth and says:

"I entreat thee by thy knees, Odysseus, and do thou show mercy on me and have pity. It will be a sorrow for thyself in the aftertime if thou slayest me who am a minstrel, and sing before gods and men."

Thereupon there follow several extremely instructive lines, concerning the view of himself as an artist which was held by the poet of the Twenty-second Book of the *Odyssey:*

"Yea, none has taught me but myself, and the god has put into my heart all manner of lays, and methinks I sing to thee as to a god, wherefore be not eager to cut off my head."

And Telemachus warmly defends and protects the poet. In other words, the poet is here glorifying himself.

When Odysseus has arrived at the land of the Phæacians, another poet is introduced into the hall of the king, a poet who is blind by virtue of the old tradition handed down from the *Iliad* and from the Homeric *Hymn to Apollo,* or perhaps of older origin than either the *Iliad* or the *Hymn:*

"Then the henchman drew near, leading with him the beloved minstrel, whom the muse loved dearly, and she gave him both good and evil; of his sight she reft him, but granted him sweet song."

In the scene with Demodocus, it is particularly striking to note how eager is the poet of the Eighth Book to impress his hearers with the proper mode of entertaining an inspired minstrel.

First, Demodocus is offered a seat on a chair with silver nails (placed against a pillar in the midst of the circle of guests); thereupon the resounding lyre is suspended from a peg over his head, so that he may seize it as the spirit moves him to do so:

"And close by him he placed a basket, and a fair table, and a goblet of wine by his side, to drink when his spirit bade him."

But that is not all. When he is again ready to sing, having been led out by the henchman and honored by those present, it is Odysseus who sees to it that his wants are not neglected:

"Then to the henchman spoke Odysseus of many counsels, for he had cut off a portion of the chine of a white-toothed boar, whereon yet more was left, with rich fat on either side: 'Lo, henchman, take this mess, and hand it to Demodocus, that he may eat, and I will bid him hail, despite my sorrow. For minstrels from all men on earth get their meed of honor and worship; inasmuch as the muse teacheth them the paths of song, and loveth the tribe of minstrels.' "

When Demodocus sings for the first time, we again find a tradition from the Trojan War, a tradition not found in the epic poems as we have them:

"The muse stirred the minstrel to sing the songs of famous men, even that lay whereof the fame had reached the wide heaven, namely, the quarrel between Odysseus and Achilles, son of Peleus; how once on a time they contended in fierce words at a rich festival of the gods, but Agamemnon, king of men, was only glad when the noblest of the Achæans fell at variance."

During the singing of this song, in which the name of Odysseus is mentioned repeatedly, while Odysseus himself is sitting unknown among the listening Phæacians, he hides his head in his cloak, and draws his hood over his head in order to conceal his flowing tears. The king—without knowing the reason—feels that the song disturbs his guest and stops its recital.

Later, dance music is played, and the minstrel sings for the dance the charming, now so celebrated, ballad concerning the taking by surprise of the two entwined lovers by Hephaistus, a song which, with its light and merry treatment of an illicit love episode, appears to be one of the later parts of the great poem. The most amusing portion is probably the passage in which Apollo asks Hermes whether he would be willing, like Ares, to expose himself to being caught in a net for the privilege of sharing Aphrodite's couch, and Hermes answers:

"I would that this might be, Apollo, my prince of archery! So might thrice as many bands innumerable encompass me about, and all ye gods be looking on and all the goddesses, yet would I lie by golden Aphrodite."

We learn from the *Odyssey* that poets were even *imported* from abroad. Thus we read, when Antinous accuses Eumæus of having invited such a beggar as Odysseus:

"For who ever himself seeks out and bids to the feast a stranger from afar, save only one of those that are craftsmen of the people, a prophet or a healer of ills, or a shipwright, or even a godlike minstrel, who can delight with his song?"

From the same (the Seventeenth) Book, we learn that in those days it was impossible to imagine a festival without the lyre and without lyric poetry:

"For the savor of the fat rises upward, and the voice of the lyre is heard there, which the gods have made to be the mate of the feast."

And even the swineherd cannot find a better comparison, in order to explain to Penelope the magic exercised by the recital of his strange guest, than that with the effect of poetry:

"Even as when a man gazes on a singer, whom the gods have taught to sing words of yearning joy to mortals, and they have a ceaseless desire to hear him, so long as he will sing, even so he charmed me, sitting by me in the halls."

The minstrel occupied a much respected social position in the days of Odysseus, as may be inferred from Nestor's narration (III, 265) that Agamemnon, at the time of his departure, had asked a minstrel who lived in the house to look after his (Agamemnon's) wife. It is of great interest to note also that in the Seventh Book, Demodocus is designated simply as the divine singer (verse 359).

But most significant is the passage in which Demodocus (VIII, 469–520) in his song tells the tale of the capture of Troy by Odysseus, with the aid of the horse fashioned of wood—unquestionably a legend that sprang from a very child-like imagination. For it is this song that melts the heart of Odysseus in the poem, and that serves as the immediate cause for his making himself known to the people of the Phæacians.

In the course of time, the high esteem in which the poet-singer stood in the *Odyssey* may have changed not a little. In Xenophon's *Memor-*

abilia, we find the rhapsodists enjoying slight esteem, being considered as of little intelligence (*Memorabilia* IV, 2), somewhat like the tenors of our own day. The memories of these poets must still have been very good—more than four centuries after the Homeric era—as we may learn from Xenophon's *Symposium* (III) in which the young Nikeratos is capable of reciting the entire *Iliad* and the entire *Odyssey,* when requested to do so by his father. It is mentioned that the rhapsodists also knew epics by heart, but someone asks the question: "Do you know any group of men more stupid than the rhapsodists?" And we read the answer: "I know of no such group."

Actors, peculiarly enough, frequently became famous, but never rhapsodists. In Plato's *Io,* a rhapsodist imagines that he has become a great general by reading Homer, for he considers generalship and the art of the rhapsodist to be one and the same thing.

We learn from Plato's *Republic* that the greatest and most artistic prose writer of Greece went so far as to cherish a hatred for all the fine arts, particularly for poets and poetry. Though Plato is far from any inclination to overestimate the Sophists, he nevertheless places the Sophists in his

Republic far above the poets. The Sophists at least made an effort to *enlighten* men. Homer and Hesiod, on the other hand, were capable of nothing but an *imitation* of the phenomena of the earth, of affording mere shadow pictures of precious things, and in reality, pursued no higher object than that of amusing or entertaining. Therefore, they rightly attained no higher estate than that of mendicant rhapsodists, or, to quote Plato literally: "Do you believe that Homer's or Hesiod's contemporaries, had these men really been able to develop their contemporaries into worthy persons, would have permitted these, their masters, to journey from town to town in order to sing?"

Plato, somewhat in the same manner as Leo Tolstoy in our day, was seized—in his moral enthusiasm—with a kind of hatred for art, and since he believes in ancient legends because he lives in an uncritical age, he imagines that Homer and Hesiod traveled from court to court, two ragged rhapsodists, in order to display their art. A whole world lies between the Homeric conception of the poetic art and that of Plato.

The *Odyssey* suffers somewhat from a shifting of the motive forces. We may observe such a shifting of motives even in the *Iliad,* although the poem in the course of time has assumed a finality of form.

Originally it is only the rape of Briseis that causes the rage of Achilles. Later—the reason is not clear—Achilles' wrath against Agamemnon is forgotten and is replaced by his anger at Hector for having slain Patroklos, his closest friend. But since this slaying is due only to the fact that Achilles has kept out of the battle owing to his hatred for Agamemnon, Agamemnon is the ultimate cause of Patroklos' death also. And yet, Achilles' hatred of Agamemnon has long been dead.

We observe traces in the *Odyssey* which show that originally it was Athene who served as the hero's enemy and prevented his return home. But from the moment when, in the Ninth Book, Odysseus has gouged out the eye of Poseidon's son, the man-eating Polyphemos, Poseidon becomes the successor of Athene as the persecutor of Odysseus. It is evident that two different cycles of legends have here become interwoven. But a third cycle also intervenes. In the Twelfth Book, Odysseus has acquired a new divine enemy, the sun itself, the god Helios.

Odysseus had been strictly forbidden to make sacrifices, *i. e.,* to slaughter and consume the oxen and cows sacred to the god of the sun. Odysseus therefore forbade his men to do so. But a very awkward poet has caused Odysseus to leave his crew, "in order to pray to the blessed gods," which he might have done without changing his position. Thereupon Odysseus falls asleep, and immediately his followers violate his express prohibition; they slaughter the sun-god's most excellent oxen.

Immediately Lampetie, daughter of Helios, hastens to the sun to bring the news, which would appear to be unnecessary, since the sun beholds all things. The sun thereupon calls upon Zeus for revenge upon the audacious men, with the droll threat that he will else descend to the underworld and shine only for the dead. The outcome is that Zeus shatters the bark of Odysseus with his shining thunderbolt.

This passage is quite childish and one of the most awkward in the *Odyssey.* Silly miracles are not found in any other part of Homer. Not even the miracles of Circe are stupid or crude. But the miracle that serves as a preliminary warning of the wrath of the gods over sacrilege is ridiculous to the point of burlesque. The flayed skins of the oxen begin to creep; the meat roasting on the spit begins to roar:

"And soon thereafter the gods showed forth signs and wonders to my company. The skins were creeping, and the flesh bellowing upon the spits, both the roast and raw, and there was a sound as the voice of kine."

Indeed, the whole story is like a children's fairy tale.

While the *Iliad* is essentially heroic, the *Odyssey* may be called a mixture of childishness and acumen.

Odysseus is the central personage; he fills the scene entirely. In all probability, the main outlines of his character were already available not only in the *Iliad,* but also in the legends concerned with the interval between the *Iliad* and the *Odyssey.* For, in the *Iliad,* where he is only brave and cunning, we find no justification for the epithet so frequently associated with him in this poem: much-tested (*polytlas*). Even the oldest of the poets of the *Odyssey* considers him to be a thoughtful man, hardened by his trials, indomitable, invulnerable to reverses, a constant source of inexhaustible strength, both in his inventiveness and in his courage.

He serves as a national Greek counterpart to Achilles. Achilles represents heroic youth with the arrogance of the born victor, and with a constantly recurring melancholy at the thought of the early death awaiting him. He gives evidence of greatness even in the First Book of the *Iliad* when he takes upon himself the protection of Kalchas: "None shall lay hands upon thee in this camp, not even the first of the men among the Achæans."

There is nothing small about his mind. He shows Agamemnon the wrong he is committing in stealing Chryseis from her father, and vows triple and quadruple retaliation against him when Troy has been conquered. Only when the king threatens him personally does his rage break forth. Youthful pride is mingled with resentment at the king's impudence: never have the Trojans done him any harm, though they have stolen his cattle; he takes up arms in the cause of his king's brother, from whom Helen has been stolen.

This is the weak point of the tale. The poet found himself obliged to take up an ancient legend which he himself obscurely felt to be unreasonable. Why in God's name should Achilles wear himself out for the sake of Menelaus? The poet represents Achilles as showing moderation, even courtesy, to the herald who takes away Chryseis. The herald is therefore without guilt. But why should he not break Agamemnon's skull? We are dealing here with a fundamental contradiction, which is due to the fact that the poet, in the *Iliad* as in the *Odyssey,* has no very clear conception of the political conditions in the days which he is describing.

These conditions are quite obscure in both these great poems. By whose decision has Agamemnon's power been made greater than that of Achilles, since Achilles also is an independent king? Why does Achilles content himself with passive resistance—which after all is the resort of the impotent and weakly—in spite of his impetuous and passionate nature?

The case is similar in the *Odyssey*. We have no indication of the nature of the royal power. Odysseus appears to be not an elected king, but an hereditary king; yet his father still lives when Odysseus returns home after an absence of twenty years. Has Laertes never been king; or wherefor has he abdicated to Odysseus while still alive? Why is he not *now* king on the island of Ithaka? Why has he not at least assumed the dignity of king during his son's absence? Why has he not faced the suitors with the dignity of his superior position? Why has he contented himself, like Voltaire's Candide, with cultivating his garden?

The legend may not have permitted these things. And Odysseus, unlike Achilles, is not passive, but merely patient. He does not give himself up to resignation, but is possessed with a profoundly human ambition, that of again beholding and taking charge of his home. His eyes look for Ithaka, for his hearth, during his journey. He develops all his abilities with this object in view, thus becoming a general human type similar to the Robinson Crusoe of an epoch that was to ensue after twenty centuries or more, and who also represents an abridged history of the human spirit. He laments when the tempest throws him out of his course and he is in danger of drowning. He then wishes that he lay dead on the plains of Troy, for there he would have had an honorable grave. He shows a respectful cheerfulness in the presence of Nausikaa, dignity in the presence of the Phæacian king and queen, and displays the strength of his body and his ability in sports in the presence of their men. He contents himself with the modest couch and the frugal food with which the goodly swineherd is able to supply him. He calmly observes the suitors reveling in his palace and (like the *einherjer* in Valhalla) consuming a whole swine each day. He shows strength of spirit and self-domination when obliged to disguise himself in the presence of his friends and servants as well as of his enemies.

When he is derided and beaten in his own house by the goatherd, by Antinous, even by the beggar Irus, his self-control remains admirable.

All the more powerful is the effect later of the wild outburst of his thirst for revenge: "Ye dogs!" No doubt they all opened their eyes wide!

The poet in this poem (as in *Robinson Crusoe*) never loses sight of the universal human quality. The trials of Odysseus are a concentrated expression of the trials that many must bear. Odysseus affords us an encouraging example of combined intelligence and energy.

If we compare the *Odyssey,* in its present shape, with the *Iliad,* we find the chief difference in form to be that narration now assumes the place occupied by action in the *Iliad*. The language is entirely the same. Nor is the form of narration strikingly different in the two poems. But the spirit has changed entirely.

We do not find in the *Odyssey* the same warlike

spirit as in the *Iliad*. Even where the material afforded an opportunity for an increased use of tension, the possibilities available are not utilized to the full, partly because of the poet's predilection for bathetic, declining episodes, and partly because of the aversion of the period to the representation of erotic passion. The reader will recall, for example, how tame is the treatment of the reunion of Odysseus and Penelope, although this reunion is the central theme of the entire work. The *Odyssey* has more unity of composition than the *Iliad,* although even the latter is quite transparent in its construction. The feasible length of the recital of a song was probably the element determining the length of the sections of both poems; but while the power of imagination displayed in the *Odyssey* is perhaps somewhat weaker, its art is all the greater. That an interval of time elapses between the two epics is shown if only by the fact that in the *Iliad* Iris is the messenger of the gods throughout, a function assumed by Hermes in the *Odyssey.* In both poems we find unnecessary interventions by the gods, for instance, when Patroklos' funeral pyre is slow to kindle in the Twenty-third Book of the *Iliad,* and Achilles therefore prays to two of the gods of the winds, and Iris, obliged to intervene for so slight a cause, finds the gods of the winds feasting at table in the hall of the West Wind, swept by a great gale, and induces them to fan the flames of the pyre.

But such superfluous uses of a goddess as an instrument are found twenty times as frequently in the *Odyssey,* in which Athene is made to act for so insignificant a purpose as that of showing her favorite the way to the palace in the city of the Phæacians (a thing that any child in town, according to the statement of the king's daughter herself, might have done), or even to exert herself in so slight a task as that of finding a hiding place for the gifts brought by Odysseus from the island of the Phæacians, after his arrival at Ithaka. She even hides the things herself in a cave for him, and places a stone at the entrance to the cave, with her own hands, as a protection against thieves, in order that Odysseus may sleep undisturbed during the night.

In the early portion of the *Odyssey,* the first four books, the last part of the work to be composed, Pallas Athene—the goddess of machines—is constantly running errands. In the very first book she is present while the suitors are amusing

and, like wide-awake children, to be instructed with tales of remote lands and their history.

The *Odyssey* may be divided into three parts. The first four books, the *Telemachia,* the narration of the itinerary of Telemachus in his visits to the heroes of the *Iliad,* to the courts of Nestor and Menelaus, were created only for the purpose of serving as a transition from the *Iliad* to the *Odyssey,* and are in reality merely a sort of padding without any value of their own. One of these books, the First, is even so poor that it cannot be considered as much more than a random selection from the following books.

Certain portions of these four books, though they are merely a stop-gap, when considered as a whole, have a certain poetic and archæological value. It is possible to trace some of the sources from which these books have been patched together. Mentes and Mentor appear to be one and the same person, bearing two names. Everything is in confusion. While it is demanded and expected elsewhere in the poem that the wooer shall give rich gifts to the bride, we find mention here of the fact that grave difficulty is encountered at

Penelope's wedding in providing the necessary equipment and a plentiful dowry. The times have changed, customs with them. Telemachus, for the rest a youth without any sharply defined traits, is here stupid enough to announce in advance to his enemies, the suitors, just what he is going to do to them (I, 386 *et seq.*), as if it were his object to prevent the accomplishment of these deeds.

In these cantos, the reminiscence of the slaying of Agamemnon by Ægisthus and Clytemnestra is still strong, although this tale has nothing to do with the action of the poem.

In the Fourth Book, we become acquainted with the fair Helen in the new situation of a worthy mother-in-law, marrying off her daughter. Helen is here acquainted with the use of magic potions, imparting sorrow and grief, with a sort of hasheesh producing good spirits in the partaker, even though he may suddenly have lost his father, mother, brother, or a beloved son. The tales she tells appear to be taken from poetic works that have since been lost, from the *Nostoi,* and from the so-called *Little Iliad.* It is surprising to find this woman, always an object of respect and esteem, in her capacity as the wife of Menelaus—which makes her a Greek woman—appearing here, in her husband's narration of the entrance of the famous wooden horse into Troy, as the enemy of the Greeks. She tries to induce them to make their presence known, as they sit hidden in the horse's body:

"Thrice thou didst go round the hollow ambush and handle it, calling aloud on the chiefs of the Argives by name, and making thy voice like the voices of the wives of all the Argives."

But all this is of no avail, since the wily Odysseus obliges his friends to sit as still as mice inside the horse's body, but very palpably this incident flows from a source of which we have no other indication.

The composition itself is here as confused as the contents. Telemachus has extraordinary difficulties, joyfully receives splendid gifts as a guest on his departure, and thereupon remains in Sparta for a whole month, without any reasonable cause, before he seriously thinks of setting out. In the Fifteenth Book, we have a literal repetition of the parting scene that has already appeared in the Fourth Book.

The second section of the *Odyssey* is the multicolored account of the hero's journeys before his return home. This section begins with the beginning of the Fifth Book and ends several hundred lines after the opening of the Thirteenth.

The third, most dramatic section of the *Odyssey,* is devoted to Odysseus's sojourn on the Island of Ithaka, extending from verse 185 of the Thirteenth Book, to the end of the poem, including therefore the Twenty-fourth Book also. Even the most ancient critics were well aware, however, that the original *Odyssey* ended with the reunion of the hero with Penelope. What remains is a later addition.

While in the *Iliad* many various destinies of individuals rival each other in importance, the figure of Odysseus is the most impressive of the male characters in the *Odyssey.*

However, there are a number of men with clearly defined outlines: Odysseus's son, Telemachus, and his father Laertes; besides, figures taken over from the *Iliad,* such as Menelaus and Nestor; furthermore Alcinous, the noble-minded king of the Phæacians; the impudent young noble, Antinoos the wooer; the goodly swineherd, Eumæus; Achilles' son serving as a thrale; and finally, the marvelous giant, the Cyclops Polyphemos.—One thing should not fail to be pointed out. There is as little development of character in the *Odyssey* as in the *Iliad*. Growth of character in the modern sense is not found until four centuries later, in the person of Neoptolemos, in the *Philoktetes* of Sophocles, or in the principal persons in the *Iphigenia* of Euripides.

Women are more numerous than in the *Iliad*. Helen appears in chastened form; Penelope dominates the entire poem with her fidelity to her absent husband; Queen Arete is depicted with a few strokes as the dominant member of the ruling pair in the kingdom of the Phæacians; anyone who has won her over has gained everything, even the king. Her daughter, Nausikaa, the only young girl in Homer, is the most splendid of all the female figures, proud and yet quite outspoken, modest and yet free in her manner. She has mental delicacy, charm, kindness, and, though she is shy, she has the temerity of a king's daughter. She is both dignified and wise, kind to the strange ship-wrecked man, and not without sympathy for his admirable and winsome qualities, but careful from the very first moment lest she be seen together with him and thus give rise to gossip. She is able to explain everything to Odysseus. Thus, she arranges that he is not to accompany her to the city.

"Their ungracious speech it is that I would avoid, lest some man afterward rebuke me, and there are but too many insolent folk among the people. And some of the baser sort might greet me and say: 'Who is this that goes with Nausikaa, this tall and goodly stranger? Where found she him? Her husband will he be, her very own. Either she has taken in some ship-wrecked wanderer of strange men,—for no men dwell near us; or some god has come in answer to her instant prayer; from heaven has he descended, and will have her to wife for evermore. Better so, if herself she has ranged abroad and found a lord from a strange land, for verily she holds in no regard the Phæacians here in this country, the many and noble men who are her wooers.' "

Nausikaa's disappointment on learning that Odysseus, whom she had wished to make her husband, has long been married, is very delicately suggested. On seeing him for the last time she merely declares that he must not forget her, since it is she to whom he owes his ability to depart for home, and she is not present when he takes leave of the land.

The description of Nausikaa is all the more meritorious when we recall that she obviously is not a figure contained in the original legend, but is the result only of the poet's acquaintance with the most distinguished young women of his day, and of his own delicate imagination.

Among Odysseus's adventures on his journey, the first to be related is his stay in the cave with the fair nymph and goddess, Calypso, the oldest prototype of the irresistible Alcinas and Armidas of Ariosto and Tasso. She holds Odysseus captive for no less than seven years. Odysseus appears, therefore, much less faithful than Penelope, and when he finally expresses the desire to leave Calypso, it is less for any longing to be home again than—as he admits—because he has become surfeited with the caresses so tirelessly lavished upon him by the sublime goddess.

> "And his eyes were never dry of tears, and his sweet life was ebbing away as he mourned for his return; for the nymph no more found favor in his sight."

Yet Calypso is at bottom more a woman than a goddess. But the treatment of erotic passions is so little favored by the Homeric style that when Hermes appears with a message from Zeus ordering Calypso to release her lover she obeys without murmur or lament. Her complaint is but short:

"Hard are ye gods and jealous exceeding, whoever grudge goddesses openly to mate with men, if any make a mortal her dear bed-fellow."

She spends but one more night in the cave with Odysseus, whereupon she equips him most solicitously with garments scented with incense, furnishes him with dark red wine, fresh water, and a bag full of foodstuffs, to be consumed on his journey, and permits him to depart.

It is interesting to note how the poet has been at an effort to give of his best—yet without resorting to any exaggerated or fantastic figures—in his description of the cave in which the goddess dwells:

"And on the hearth there was a great fire burning, and from afar through the isle was smelt the fragrance of cleft cedar blazing, and of sandal wood. And the nymph within was singing with a sweet voice as she fared to and fro before the loom, and wove with a shuttle of gold. And round about the cave there was a wood blossoming, alder and poplar and sweet-smelling cypress. And therein roosted birds long of wing, owls and falcons and chattering sea-crows, which have their business in the waters. And lo, there about the hollow cave trailed a gadding garden vine, all rich with clusters. And fountains four set orderly were running with clear water, hard by one another, turned each to his own course. And all around soft meadows bloomed of violets and parsley."

This is the veritable Garden of Eden in its original Greek form.—A rather amusing passage is that in which Calypso, after having relinquished her claims on Odysseus, expresses some surprise at his preferring Penelope to her, although he has not seen Penelope for twenty years:

"Not in sooth that I avow me to be less noble than she in form or fashion, for it is in no wise meet that mortal women should match them with immortals, in shape and comeliness."

Odysseus very tactfully concedes the point made by the goddess:

"Myself I know it well, how wise Penelope is meaner to look upon than thou, in comeliness and stature. But she is mortal and thou knowest not age nor death. Yet even so, I wish and long day by day to fare homeward and see the day of my returning."

Among the few scenes in the *Odyssey* that are not merely entertaining, but may be called truly impressive, there is, in addition to the slaying of the suitors at the end of the epic, the famous and admirable picture of the storm that overwhelms Odysseus's raft after his parting with Calypso. This is the work of a master. Everything is indicated here in a few powerful strokes, and with undeviating sureness of touch. We here have a treatment of Odysseus's changing emotions, depression, the return of his strength of will, despair, resolution, heroic energy, entreaty, a burst of joy and confidence. The description is shot through with the most original comparisons. When Odysseus has been dashed overboard by a great sea, and has finally spat out the salt water from his lungs and once more is sitting on a plank, we read:

"And the great wave swept it hither and thither along the stream. And as the North Wind in the harvest tide sweeps the thistle-down along the plain, and close the tufts cling to each other, even so the winds bare the raft hither and thither along the main."

When Odysseus, with the advice and aid of the mermaid Leukothea, who presents herself to him in the shape of a cormorant, has finally come to the point of glimpsing land in the distance after two days and nights of wretchedness, we have the artistic lines:

"And even as when most welcome to his children is the sight of a father's life, who lies in sickness and strong pains long wasting away, some angry god assailing him; and to their delight the gods have loosed him from his trouble; so welcome to Odysseus showed land and wood; and he swam onward being eager to set foot on the strand."

A foamy wave casts him ashore on the stony beach, and—though I may be tiring the reader with quotations—I must yet bring to his attention the poet's precision in his description of the condition of Odysseus's hands:

"And as when the cuttle-fish is dragged forth from his chamber, the mossy pebbles clinging to his suckers, even so was the skin stript from his strong hands against the rocks, and the great wave closed over him."

Beginning with the moment when Odysseus feels the land under his feet on the island of the Phæacians and after the episode with Nausikaa, the *Odyssey* assumes an entirely new tone. When the poem was put into its final artistic form, the editor—whoever he may have been—hit upon the device of having the tale of Odysseus's numerous journeys, during the many years that had preceded, related by the hero himself in the royal hall of the Phæacians. This makes the *Odyssey*—although it obviously was gathered into a single epic only because the *Iliad* had been so formulated—a more compact and lucidly constructed composition. The fact that some editing has taken place, that the stories were not originally related by Odysseus himself but narrated in the third person, is rather easy to prove.

Odysseus here is constantly aware of things that he really should not know. For instance, he falls asleep while approaching Ithaka, and yet he knows the things said by the sailors to each other while he is sleeping (X, 38–46).—Although he has never been in the land of the Lestrygons, he knows the name of the Lestrigon Antiphates and of the beautiful spring Artakia, names that have not been communicated to him by anyone.

At times, the editor has made a crude effort to remedy this difficulty. When, in the Twelfth Book, Odysseus has narrated an entire conversation between Lamphetie and Zeus, a conversation of which Odysseus should know nothing, the following naïve lines are inserted as a sort of later patch:

"This I heard from Calypso of the fair hair; and she said that she herself had heard it from Hermes the messenger,"

an extremely unpoetic expression.

Odysseus, in telling his story, knows of the conversation between his men while they were standing outside Circe's house (X, 212), while he himself was absent, and he mentions again and again the youth who advised him as to the method of resisting the charms of Circe, as the god Hermes, although it is expressly stated that the god did not make himself known to Odysseus, but appeared in human form. All the contradictions in these matters disappear if we assume these tales to have been orginally narrated not by Odysseus but by the poet. For it is naturally the poet's right—nay, his duty—to be omniscient. The passages pointed out show that the attempt to impart a more close-knit quality to the composition of the *Odyssey* has been carried out with considerable carelessness. Furthermore, it may be noted in general that Homer frequently has his persons pronounce words addressed to the attention of Homer's hearers and not of their own hearers.

In the Tenth Book of the *Odyssey,* which is full of adventures, we feel the influence of contemporary, or rather older, poems concerning the Argonautic expedition, poems since lost. Thus we find the legend of the island of Æolus, which floats upon the sea surrounded by a wall of copper; concerning Æolus himself, who holds the roaring winds captive in a sack prepared by himself of the hide of an ox nine years old; the legend of the land where the nights are bright in summer, as in Denmark. It does not seem probable that Denmark is meant, since no Greek ever reached so far north before the days of Pytheas of Marseilles, five centuries after the origin of the *Odyssey*. But we may nevertheless be dealing with a legend concerning our own bright nights, since the Phœnicians visited our waters for the purpose of purchasing amber and trading with it in foreign climes, and the Phœnicians may have informed the marveling Greeks of the quality of these nights. We read the words:

"The Lestrygons, where herdsman hails herdsman as he drives in his flock, and the other who drives forth answers the call. There might a sleepless man have earned a double wage, the one as neat-herd, the other shepherding white flocks: so near are the outgoings of the night and of the day."

As already stated, much seems to have been taken from the legend of the Argonauts. The spring Artakia, which is mentioned, was not mythical but real, being situated near the town of Cyzikos, and being mentioned in the account of the founding of Miletos, occurring again in the tale of the Argonautic voyages.—The island of Aiaia, on which Circe dwells, also lies in this region, and Circe, the fair-haired sorceress of this island, is also taken from the legend of the Argonauts. When we read the express words (X, 137):

"An awful goddess of mortal speech, own sister to the wizard Æetes,"

this means that she is a sister to one of the Argonautic heroes, the king of Colchis. For this reason we find another reference, later in the *Odyssey,* to the ship *Argo.* In the description of the dangerous, rocky cliffs (XII, 70), which—by the way —are identical with the Symplegades, said to have been a source of so much woe to the Argonauts, we read:

"One ship only of all that fare by sea hath passed that way, even the far-famed Argo, that is in all men's minds, on her voyage from Æetes."

Our translation puts it: *the far-famed.* A more literal translation would be: *the much-sung,* making it clear that our *Odyssey* has absorbed not a little of the material of the Argonautic epic. Circe had transformed the Argonauts into bears and tigers before transforming the men in the *Odyssey* into swine. She appears to this extent less original than Calypso, who may hardly be found anywhere else than in the *Odyssey.* In Homer, Circe is unique in her practise of magic. She has her charm and is far more dæmonic than the merely lovesick Calypso.—Quite amusing is her change of heart when she, accustomed to turn all men into ridiculous beasts through the use of her magic wand, encounters in the person of Odysseus him who is destined to be her lord and master. Hermes gives Odysseus the root called *môly* by the gods, which wards off all witchcraft. When Circe, after uttering the words:

"Go thy way now to the stye; couch thee there with the rest of thy company," strikes him with her wand, he draws his sharp battle sword upon her. She thereupon bursts out with her declaration that her magic potions usually have the effect of depriving men of their will power:

"But thou hast, methinks, a mind within thee that may not be enchanted. Verily thou art Odysseus, ready at need, whom he of the golden wand, the slayer of Argos, full often told me was to come hither, on his way from Troy with his swift black ship. Nay come, put thy sword into the sheath, and thereafter let us go up into my bed, that meeting in love and sleep we may each trust the other."

The concluding request for absolute confidence is a little striking, coming as it does from a lady of Circe's type. But possibly she may resemble other women also in being accommodating to them who possess the magic root which, according to Hermes, is called *môly* by the gods. Its name in the language of humans is unfortunately not communicated.—In her hands, Odysseus forgets everything, even his resoluteness, with the result that he is unable to tear himself away until expressly summoned to do so by his men. As sister to Æetes, this dangerous nymph is a counterpart to her brother's daughter Medea, who plays such a prominent part in the legend of the Argonauts.—Circe did not become a subject of sculpture until a much later day. The so called wall of Kypselos shows her embracing Odysseus, and the rule of the Kypselides in Corinth does not begin until 680 B. C.

As the poem concerning the shield of Achilles, found in the *Iliad,* is a beautiful and instructive interpolation, which existed before the events justifying its use, so the story of the Cyclops Polyphemus is one of the oldest portions of the work, an independent little folk-poem, obviously of much greater age, as a first-class story for children.

The poet perhaps made use of an early song as a basis. The childish invention according to which Odysseus, foreseeing a possible later situation, calls himself *Nobody,* might point in this direction. The Cyclops is a remarkably living figure. He is a cannibal and abhors men except as a foodstuff, but he cannot be considered a prototype for Shakespeare's Caliban, since his bestial behavior is softened by his kindly attitude toward animals, his affection for his herd.

We are here probably dealing with the popular bugbear, the man-eating and child-eating giant;

but he is none the less a living creature, not repellent to our imagination, and captivating us with his half-animal soul in spite of the terror he inspires.

Marvelous are the lines which tell of the manner in which Odysseus's men deprive the Cyclops of his vision:

"For their part they seized the bar of olive wood, that was sharpened at the pont, and thrust it into his eye, while I from my place aloft turned it about, as when a man bores a ship's beam with a drill while his fellows below spin it with a strap, which they hold at either end, and the auger runs round continually."

That the story of the Cyclops is an independent section, in spite of its masterly execution, is apparent from a single glance at the concise account of the contents of the *Odyssey* given by Aristotle in his *Poetics:*

"A man is absent from home for many years and Poseidon keeps his eyes upon him constantly. He is alone. The conditions at his home include a devastation of his property and an attempt to destroy his son. Now he returns home, beaten out of his course by a storm, again recognizes certain persons and issues commands to them, delivers himself and lays low his enemies."

It would appear to be high time for us to arrive at a discussion of what is stated to be the true subject of the *Odyssey* in this laconic declaration by Aristotle.

But we must still dwell for a moment on a captivating and extraordinary interpolation in the narration of Odysseus before he says farewell to the Phæacians. One of the poets, possibly the author of the Twelfth Book, yielded to a desire to narrate the great wanderer's descent to the realm of the dead. And in order to provide a pretext for this interpolation, he has Circe command Odysseus to put questions to the prophet Tiresius, who has long been dead, to obtain advice from Tiresius as to Odysseus's return home. There is no good reason for Circe's sending Odysseus to Hades, nor does Tiresius give him any particularly useful information.

But the temptation to describe the life of the dead beneath the soil has always been attractive to the imagination of ancient and modern times. In the Sixth Book of the *Æneid,* as is well known, Virgil imitates the Eleventh Book of the *Odyssey,* and Dante also permitted himself to be influenced by Virgil, whom he therefore makes his guide.

The Eleventh Book, the *Nekyia,* contains a number of fine things. Even the fundamental notion that the erring shades obtained a semblance of life by drinking the blood that flows from sacrificed lambs, is a good one, also the necessity to which Odysseus is put, to hold the shades at bay with his drawn sword. The conversation between Odysseus and his deceased mother is very neat. She knows of the lonely life of Laertes in the country, but is not aware of the state of things in the palace. She did not die, according to her story, of sudden pestilence or of illness,

"such as chiefly with a sad wasting draws the spirit from the limbs; nay, it was my sore longing for thee, and for thy counsels, great Odysseus, and for thy loving-kindness, that reft me of sweet life."

This conversation is followed by a tedious encounter with a number of distinguished women of antiquity. This entire passage, about one hundred and fifty verses, hardly belongs to this place, can hardly have been written by any of the Homeric poets, and probably emanates from some Bœotian or Hesiodic source.

Then Agamemnon steps forth and reports to Odysseus the tragedy of his home-coming, the tale of Agamemnon's murder while banqueting in his own hall, by Ægisthus in coöperation with Queen

Clytemnestra, "as an ox is slaughtered at his crib." It is no cause for surprise to find that Agamemnon, after suffering this treatment, expresses the same views of women as are found in Euripides, Schopenhauer, Eduard von Hartmann, and Strindberg:

"So surely is there nought more terrible and shameless than a woman who imagines such evil in her heart."

Quite amusing is the good advice he gives Odysseus as to the proper treatment of women. He is well aware of Penelope's righteousness, but he admonishes him:

"Wherefore do thou too, never henceforth be soft even to thy wife, neither show her all the counsel that thou knowest, but a part declare and let part be hid."

Then follows the meeting with the shade of Achilles, who receives this homage from Odysseus:

"For of old, in the days of thy life, we Argives gave thee one honour with the gods, and now thou art a great prince here among the dead."

When Achilles answers him with an obviously unconquerable melancholy, Odysseus attempts to console him by telling of the reputation for invulnerability held by his son Neoptolemus.

The lament of Achilles is a wonderful piece of work. When Ajax appears after the disappearance of Achilles, we are given in firm strokes a description of Ajax's gloomy rage on being worsted in the competition when Odysseus won from him the armor of Achilles.

Respectful and friendly though the manner of Odysseus's approach to Ajax, the latter answers him not a word, but mutely turns his back upon him and disappears. I consider this incident to be overwhelming in its discreet artistry.

The following portion is a quite insignificant addition made at a much later day. After first declaring that the shades are tenuous and lack consciousness, one poet serves us with a great mass of idle, mythical material. The scenes depicted here from the interior of Hades could surely not have been observed by Odysseus from his position at the entrance. While the other deceased persons lack any sensual perceptions, we suddenly find, in contradiction with the description of the plain on which the shades appear in their ascent from Erebos, that Minos rushes out, seated upon his judgment seat, accompanied by the fettered Titan Tityos, Tantalus languishing in his swamp, and Sisyphus laboring on his rocky slope. The careless method of this interpolation is best indicated by the following line:

> "But I abode there still, if perchance some one of the hero folk besides might come, who died in old time,"

which clearly refers to the situation ensuing immediately after the disappearance of Ajax.

The immediate object in the *Odyssey* is to get the hero back home to Ithaka; the ultimate and basic object is to restore him as master in his own house.

For a long time it was assumed that the island of Thiaki was identical with the island called Ithaka in antiquity. A number of investigators, of whom Wilhelm Dörpfeld is the most convincing and fundamental, have succeeded in proving that the island of Leukas in the Ionian Sea is the only island fully answering the descriptions given in Homer of Ithaka. It is particularly important to note its easy access to the continent, so that in ancient times it was possible to reach land from the northeastern coast of the island by means of a ferry (*Odyssey* XX, 27), or—in our day—over an isthmus of land. Even to this day the number of pigs on the island is very large!

As opposed to the many scholars who, like Wilamowitz, have considered Homer's geography to be purely fictitious, Dörpfeld has successfully shown that the four Achaian islands which are repeatedly mentioned are the four islands off the west coast of Greece, now bearing the names of Leukas, Thiaki, Kephalenia, and Zakynthos. Of these, Leukas was the Ithaka of antiquity. The little island of Asteris, which is also mentioned, is the Arkudi of the present day.

From the moment of the landing of Odysseus, the composition in the last twelve books is very compact. We again find Odysseus not recognized, leading his idyllic life with the faithful swineherd. Then comes the scene in which Telemachus and Odysseus recognize each other. Since men in those days were as primitive in their sentiments as they were naïve in their cruelty, father and son embrace each other with streams of tears and with shouts and screams of joy, after the recognition:

"And they wailed aloud, more ceaselessly than birds, sea-eagles or vultures of crooked claws, whose younglings the country folk have taken from the nest, ere yet they are fledged."

Later, Odysseus faces Penelope, still unrecognized by her. Although his long absence and his wretched clothing might seem to be enough to make it difficult to recognize who he is, the poet in addition has Athene deprive him of his rich growth of hair and make his form appear more aged and bent, that he may shine the more thereafter.

Athene now inspires Penelope with the idea of first arraying herself in her best adornments. In her own divine person, Athene bathes her, anoints her with ambrosial ointments, rouges her fair cheeks, makes her skin more dazzling than ivory, causes her to put on her best raiment, and then has her descend from the loft and present herself to the reveling suitors.

"And straightway the knees of the wooers were loosened, and their hearts were enchanted with love, and each one uttered a prayer that he might be her bed-fellow."

Now Athene, well aware that the next day will bring death to all the suitors, advises Penelope to summon them to appear on the next morning with oxen and lambs for a banquet, besides bringing splendid gifts. The primitive Penelope acquiesces in the proposition of the goddess, to the great satisfaction of the not less primitive Odysseus.

"Thus she spake, and the steadfast goodly Odysseus rejoiced because she drew from them gifts, and beguiled their souls with soothing words, while her heart was set on other things."

Thereupon, Odysseus appears as a beggar in the doorway of his own hall, now occupied by the suitors, is reviled, is smitten by the stools which are thrown at his shoulders, and is forced to engage in a hand to hand encounter with the beggar outcast Irus.

This is the moment when Penelope proposes to the suitors that they engage in competitive battles for her possession. She will belong to him who can send an arrow, using Odysseus's old bow, through the rings of twelve double axes arranged in a row in the customary manner of suspending them from the hooks provided for the purpose.

It is rather interesting to find one of the suitors use the expression:

"Wise Penelope, if all the Achæans in Iasian Argos could behold thee, even a greater press of wooers would feed in your halls from to-morrow's dawn."

This expression shows that the oldest form of the word *Ionian* was *Iaonian,* and this is interesting when we recall that Genesis x, in the enumeration of the generations of Noah's offspring, designates the Ionians with the name of *Iavan.*

Now the whole story revolves about the bow of Odysseus. All interest centers on the bow in Odysseus's hand, his simple weapon for the attainment of victory and eternal fame. This bow is in reality the bow of Eurytos. It was Eurytos who bequeathed it to Iphitos and Iphitos gave it to Odysseus before Iphitos himself was slain by his guest friend Herakles for his fine stallions. Behind this bow we glimpse a great number of ancient legends and ancient songs concerning its past history.

There are a few famous bows in ancient legend: the bow of Odysseus, the bow of Philoktetes, the bow of Einarr Thambaskelfir,[1] and the bow of William Tell, which originally belonged to Palnatoki.[2]

[1] The sources for the story of this medieval Norwegian king will be found treated in W. S. Dahl, *Ejnar Thambarskelver, et Stykke norsk Historie,* Christiania 1884.—TRANSLATOR.

[2] A Norse hero, embodying certain traits of the William Tell legend. He is best presented in the Old Norse Jómsvíkingasaga. See Eugen Mogk, *Norwegisch-isländische Literatur,*

It is a turning point in the *Odyssey* when Penelope, mistress of the house, commands the insolent suitors to permit the beggar to try whether he can stretch the bow which all the rest, with all their efforts and their attempts to soften and grease it, have been unable to do.

Odysseus has the bow in his hands! Now he is great; he is greatness itself. We here have the whole epic concentrated in a single mighty symbol. At last, after twenty years, he recovers his bow:

"He already was handling the bow, turning it every way about, and proving it on this side and on that, lest the worms might have eaten the horns when the lord of the bow was away."

The suitors observe this spectacle with wonderment:

"Even as when a man that is skilled in the lyre and in minstrelsy, easily stretches a cord about a new peg, after tying at either end the twisted sheepgut, even so Odysseus straightway bent the great bow, all without effort, and took it in his right hand and proved the bow-string, which rang sweetly at the touch, in tone like a swallow."

in Paul's *Grundriss der germanischen Philologie,* vol. ii, Strassburg, 1909.—TRANSLATOR.

He has borne all their indignities without turning an eyelid. His enemies have beset his mistress, have had their will with his slave-girls, have comported themselves as masters in his palace, have eaten for days and nights, year in, year out, they have heaped every indignity upon him, kicks and blows, and have been untiring in their derision of him.

Now he has stretched his good, rare bow, cast off his rags, and stands with royal determination on his own threshold, proud, one against many, hard as steel, as ominous and inexorable as doom itself.

And each arrow that speeds from his hands brings death with it.

Odysseus with the bow in his hands is Alexander on Bucephalus, Cæsar heading his Tenth Legion, Napoleon with his Old Guard, Demosthenes on Pnyx, Michelangelo with his chisel, Rembrandt with his pallette, Bellman [1] with his lyre, Beethoven at his piano—the man who holds in his hands the means for attaining the victory that is *his,* without which he is not himself.

The poem depicts the effect on the minds of the

[1] Carl Michael Bellman (1740–1795), a celebrated Swedish song writer of the Eighteenth Century.—TRANSLATOR.

suitors: terror, entreaty, defiance, fighting spirit. But the merciless hour of retribution has arrived:

"Ye dogs, ye said in your hearts that I should never more come home from the land of the Trojans, in that ye wasted my house."

The reader feels the poet's joy in Odysseus's unmoving and forbidding attitude, his calm inexorableness, his firm cruelty—and the poetry of revenge is present in the now impending mass execution, which gradually is carried out.

We then read of old Eurykleia's jubilation at again beholding her master, surrounded by the pierced bodies of all the slain.

We then have the jubilant house-cleaning; the floor is purified with sponges and adzes, the blood is washed from the walls of the palace, the remnants of broken tables and the wine that has been spilled, are removed—this house-cleaning, in which the slave girls who but recently consorted with the suitors are obliged to take part, while their certain death by decapitation or by hanging awaits them. Odysseus had at first condemned them to be beheaded, but Telemachus prefers to string them all up along a suspended cable.

The poet, with his more gentle leanings, softens

this judicial horror, which is hardly justifiable when viewed from the attitude of our modern view of life:

"And flung it (the cable) round the kitchen-dome, and fastened it aloft, that none might touch the ground with her feet. And even as when thrushes, long of wing, or doves fall into a net that is set in a thicket, as they seek to their roosting-place, and a hateful bed harbours them, even so the women held their heads all in a row, and about all their necks nooses were cast, that they might die by the most pitiful death. And they writhed with their feet for a little space, *but for no long while.*"

The legend was not as merciful as the poet. The impudent goatherd Melanthius is dragged from the hall into the yard:

"And they cut off his nostrils and his ears with the pitiless sword, and drew forth his vitals for the dogs to devour raw, and cut off his hands and feet in their cruel anger."

Then the entire palace is fumigated from top to bottom. Now follows a merry dance across the floor so recently covered with blood. When Hugo von Hofmannsthal in 1904 presented us with an Elektra dancing torch in hand, after Orestes has slain his mother and Ægisthus, the critics declared that this trait was entirely contrary to the spirit of antiquity.

Presumably these wise critics had never read an epic known as the *Odyssey,* and yet Greek boys and girls have been reading this book for thousands of years.

In order that the people of the city may not hear of the massacre too soon, and may not gather their forces for revenge before Odysseus has organized his own forces for resistance, the event is hidden under the cover of dancing, singing and games. The general slaughter is followed by a ballet, and the servant girls put on their finery in order to detract the attention of those about them. The minstrel seizes his resounding lyre and as he plays, a merry and inspiring choragic dance moves across the floor, now purified of the blood with which it has been sullied.

Meanwhile, the poet has worked in Penelope's recognition of Odysseus, which he follows with a reunion of the pair, as both climb into the couch fashioned long ago by Odysseus himself about the trunk of an olive tree,

"and so they came gladly to the rites of their bed, as of old."

The reunion is therefore depicted in very brief fashion. Here the oldest portion of the *Odyssey* ends. Later there was added the beautiful rural idyll which describes the meeting of Odysseus with his old father, the wild commotion among the relatives and friends of the suitors, the descent of the suitors to the realm of the dead, and Athene's final conciliation of all parties.

In the *Iliad,* which originated among the conquerors of new lands on the islands and coasts of Asia, the tone was entirely different than among those who were calmly enjoying conquered resources. We find, therefore, many idyllic oases in the *Odyssey;* therefore they have such great hearts and such great wisdom in spite of their primitive rudeness.

In this poem the fires of the heart had reached the spirit and illuminated it.

No other people presents such an impressive union of mental acumen with native enthusiasm, of genuine feeling with true delicacy, as do the ancient Greeks.

XENOPHON

IN February, 1922, I was staying at Rapallo, not far from Genoa. The sun was bright and the water fine, and beautiful colors played over the sea and the cliffs along the coast.

Having been working at Homer for about a year, I had taken some Greek books with me, and finally my entire interest centered about Xenophon's *Anabasis,* which, though I had already been acquainted with it as a boy at school, I had finally come to regard as one of the books most pregnant with wisdom and affording in a nutshell a picture of the spirit of Greek antiquity about the year 400 B. C.

The retreat of the Ten Thousand is surely not a profound book, but owing to the simple, lucid style of an eye-witness of the events narrated, it impresses upon us, in the first place, a great deed of prowess; in the second place, the Greek and Persian spirit of the times; and finally, the mode of thought of the savage or half-savage Asiatic tribes of the period.

Xenophon, the son of Gryllos, was an Athenian who lived to be eighty years old (434–354 B. C.); he was a striking beauty as a youth, and always remained a charming man, of chivalrous character, a splendid sportsman, with the blood of adventurers and princes in his veins, a man with abilities that long remained concealed from himself as well as from others. He went with an army as a mere amateur onlooker, was neither a soldier nor an officer, and yet, at the decisive moment, he turned out to be a born general. He was still a boy when Socrates met him one day in the streets of Athens, stopped him by holding out his staff before him, and asked him whether he knew where certain commodities could be obtained. The boy possessed the required information and made a neat reply. Thereupon Socrates said: "And where will you find men who are handsome and good?" (*kaloi k'aaathoi, i.e.,* highly gifted and noble-minded.) This question the boy could not answer Whereupon Socrates said: "Then follow me!" The boy complied.

Socrates had no reason to be ashamed of his pupil.

Xenophon does not reach the heights of his *Anabasis* in all of his other writings. The *Anabasis* is a book that literally overflows with the knowledge of human character. For knowledge means the ability to extract something from everything. Cyrus, brother to the Persian king Artaxerxes, had asked the Bœotian Proxenes, a friend of Xenophon, to undertake to lead an army of Greek mercenaries to his assistance in Cilicia. Proxenes asked Xenophon whether he wanted to accompany the expedition. Since the Persians had but recently been enemies to the Hellenes, Xenophon did not immediately consent to enter the service of a Persian satrap, although he heard nothing but good about Cyrus. On the other hand, he felt a keen desire to cast about a bit and gain some experiences.

He therefore asked Socrates for advice. Socrates told him to question the Oracle at Delphi. Xenophon set out for Delphi, and asked what he should do in order to make the journey contemplated by him a successful one. The Oracle answered diplomatically: "Give offering to the gods; it is the custom to give offerings in such cases." Being eager for the journey, Xenophon neglected to ask whether the journey as such should be undertaken—for which Socrates later rebuked him. Yet, it was not a bad thing for later generations that Xenophon did not permit himself to be deterred.

The first part of the story is as follows: The mendacious satrap Tissaphernes had accused Cyrus before Artaxerxes of desiring to take the life of the latter, his elder brother. Artaxerxes thereupon had Cyrus imprisoned and sentenced to death, but was moved to leniency by their mother, Parysatis, and permitted Cyrus to return to his satrapy, but now Cyrus burned for revenge and determined to carry out precisely the deed of which he had been wrongly accused. He immediately began to recruit Hellenic troops.

The Ionian cities, with the exception of Miletus, had all gone over to Cyrus. He deceived the king by forwarding all the taxes that were requested, like a true satrap.

His sole confident was the Greek general Clearchus, to whom he had given ten thousand dareiks for the recruiting of Hellenic soldiers. He alone knew that these soldiers would be used in opposition to the great king himself. No one suspected this at first, not even Proxenes or Xenophon, who believed that the war was to be waged against a restless boundary tribe, the Pisidians. Cyrus had great qualities, was high-minded, generous, brave, highly gifted. But in addition, he was cunning and he lied ceaselessly in order to conceal his purposes and objects. His army was extremely small when measured by his undertaking. His Persian troops under Ariæos were not worth very much, and his Hellenic auxiliaries amounted only to eleven thousand hoplites (heavily armed soldiers) and two thousand peltasts (light armed soldiers). The king, if allowed sufficient time to prepare himself, could put one hundred men into the field against each man of Cyrus.

When Xenophon was introduced to Cyrus in the city of Sardes, Cyrus already owed the soldiers three months' pay, and their disaffection was growing day by day. Cyrus's popularity with women now turned out to be a very valuable quality. For one fine day Epyaxa, Queen of Cilicia, the noble wife of king Syennesis, arrived in town with great sums of money for her friend Cyrus, thus enabling him to pay the soldiers in a single sum their arrears for five months.

He wished to display his Hellenic army to this generous lady. His bold soldiers were splendidly equipped. They had taken off the coverings of their shields, which shone and glistened in the sun. They wore steel helmets, purple garments, greaves, lances and swords. At the sound of the trumpet, they uttered their war cry and all dashed forward with their shields held before them.

Their manner was so warlike that Epyaxa was frightened. She jumped out of her chariot and fled. The terror spread. All the persons who had gathered at the market place left their goods in the lurch and made off. With loud laughter, the Hellenes marched back to their tents.

Epyaxa arrived in Tarsus, the capital of Cilicia, five days ahead of Cyrus. The Greek soldiers plundered the town; it is hardly surprising that Syennesis should have assumed a hostile attitude at first, but Cyrus succeeded in appeasing the husband and in making an alliance with him. Syennesis placed much money in the hands of Cyrus, and in return, according to Xenophon, obtained the gifts in which barbarians and kings delight: necklaces of gold, horses with golden bridles, a golden sword, and a Persian festive garment.

The soldiers stayed in Tarsus for three days, evincing no desire to advance. They had begun to suspect that they were to be led against the great king and had been recruited for this purpose. It is here that Clearchus showed his cleverness. He inveigled the troops by meeting them half-way;

they trusted to his honesty until it was too late.

Finally, the moment came when it was impossible to conceal the truth any longer from the soldiers. A number deserted; but most permitted themselves to be persuaded when Cyrus offered them a great increase in pay. And Xenophon does not find this to be unreasonable. Although he himself is very punctilious in financial matters, he considers it no more than right that a mercenary, a hireling, should ask as much as he can get.

When the collision took place at Cunaxa, it turned out that Cyrus's army was so small compared with that of the king, that its left wing did not even reach to the center of the king's army. Although the number of Greeks was an insignificant fraction of that of the Persians, they were, nevertheless, held in such terror that the Persians ran before them as soon as they shouted their pæans and their war cry. Of all the Greeks, who after all had neither cavalry nor chariots, the tanks of those days, only one man was wounded. Cyrus himself fought with the greatest gallantry, dispersed the royal guard of six thousand horsemen with his six hundred horsemen, and wounded his brother in the breast. But then he was himself struck in the eye by a dart, and fell. The king had his head and hands cut off and was exhibited to the public view. The Greeks, being victorious on their wing, and beholding the Persians also flee before Cyrus, imagined that the victory was certain, not learning until the next day of the death of Cyrus, and therefore of the tragic end of the entire military expedition. The Persians, who had in vain demanded that they give up their arms, at first promised them an unmolested march back to Hellas, but later determined to dispose of them by means of a base strategy. The five Greek generals were invited to an amicable conference in the tent of the Persian commander, and were there suddenly attacked. Four of them were decapitated immediately thereafter; the fifth, the most untrustworthy, was subjected to torture for a whole year before he was finally executed. The twenty captains and two hundred soldiers that had served as the escort of the five generals were cut down at the same time. A Greek officer, mortally wounded, with difficulty holding back with his hands his protruding entrails, still mounted on his horse, announced the events of the day in camp to his fellow-countrymen.

The following night, when all, despairing, indifferent, and downcast, had gone to sleep, Xenophon alone was unable to remain on his couch. He rose and awakened the soldiers to the danger and to the necessity of immediately electing generals so that they might immediately set out the next day.

He cast out from the camp with contumely an officer who spoke in favor of submission; the pierced ears of this officer showed that he was a half-Lydian. Xenophon himself, though but an amateur, was elected as one of the generals, assuming the most difficult post, namely, the command of the rear guard. He fought his way forward by day and by night, hungry and thirsty, without shelter (all the tents and carts having been burned in accordance with his instructions), fighting ceaselessly, crossing rivers, crossing mountains, in constant danger of his life, until, while he was mounting the side of Mount Thekes, on January 27, 400 B.C., he heard—he was still in command of the rear guard—strident shouts far ahead, and dashed up on horseback, fearing an ambuscade. But the cry he heard was: *"Thalassa! Thalassa!"* (The sea! The sea!) They had reached the eastern end of the south shore-line of the Black Sea. From the moment they beheld the sea, the Greeks felt they were near home, being a nation of seamen.

But they still had more than a year to travel, through dangers of every kind, subjected to constant desertions and betrayals, until finally Xenophon, in March, 399 B. C., after all his kindness to the army, maligned, disliked, hated because of trivial and untrue accusations, gave up the command and thus was deprived of the privilege of leading the Ten Thousand, now dwindled to 8,500, back to Hellas in his own person.

He did not dare go to Athens, his native city, for here his great teacher had been obliged to drink the hemlock. And Xenophon himself was in danger of incurring the death penalty as a friend of the Persians. He accordingly went to Sparta, but when Athens, in 395 B. C., made an alliance with Artaxerxes and declared war on Sparta, Xenophon, now a friend of the Spartans, was condemned to life-long banishment for his Laconian sympathies, all his goods being confiscated.

Hardly forty-one years of age, he retired from public life, and lived as a retired country gentleman and writer on a farm given him by the Spartans. His many books, of which the *Symposion,* the *Apologia,* the *Cyropædia,* and the Socratic *Memorabilia* are the best known, are books of a somewhat lower type, but the *Anabasis* is a veritable gold-mine for him who wishes to know the meaning of genius in generalship and of the passions of the mob. As the leader of the Ten Thousand, Xenophon is the knight errant of ancient Hellas, alert, inventive, more than bold, humane, far too gentlemanly to be able to handle with the necessary roughness the crude wretches whose *condottiere* he is. They could be managed by a man like Clearchus, whose hand never relinquished the chastening rod as the hand of Suvarov, more than two thousand years later, never relinquished the knout.

It is characteristic of Xenophon's antique sense of decency that, like Cæsar after him, he speaks of himself only in the third person, and characteristic of his personal modesty, that he names as the author of the *Anabasis* a certain Themistogenes of Syracuse. The *Anabasis* is striking in its repeated contrasts between the Hellenes and the Persians, the latter being distinctly termed barbarians. Every non-Hellene is a barbarian, just as every non-Israelite in Palestine was a pagan. But the image presented to us of the Persians in the *Anabasis* is quite far from our modern conception of barbarism. In fact, the picture given by Xenophon in the *Cyropædia* of the great Cyrus as youth and man is a purely Hellenized ideal image. The first Cyrus is literally bursting with virtues. All his qualities are idealized. Compare the description of his death in Herodotus, who is concise and truthful, in which Queen Tomyris has his head cut off and thrown into a skin filled with human blood so that he may finally satisfy his blood-thirsty soul, with the *lit de parade* found at the end of the *Cyropædia,* in which Cyrus, dying in his bed, delivers a speech of two hundred and twenty-five closely printed lines, full of the noblest sentiments, before he finally disposes himself to breathe his last.

In the *Cyropædia,* which is a romance, Xenophon's idealism and optimism—two dubious quantities—are made manifest. The whole work is a construction of romantic rhetoric. But in the *Anabasis* the descriptions are truthful, the experiences are the author's own, and in this work we find the Persians showing a certain monarchic refinement of character, as contrasted with the republican refinement of the Greeks.

Note this scene for instance: When the younger Cyrus is advancing, the army passes into a narrow defile, so full of mud and mire that all the wagons and carts bearing the army's provisions are obstructed and cannot be budged. Cyrus beckons to the young Persian grandees in his immediate environment; all alight swiftly from their horses, discard their purple cloaks, on the spot, and dash off as if engaged in a race. In their rich costumes, with their embroidered trousers, their precious bracelets and adornments, they all rush into the mud without hesitation, lift the vehicles from the ground, and thus free them at once from their obstructions.

Such was the manner in which the Samurai sacrificed themselves for their king in the classic days of old Japan. The modern man sees no barbarism in this, for we have seen aristocratic dandies sacrificing their splendor and their finery in their devotion to a rebellious prince.

Compare the western barbarians of the middle ages, the Goths, the Alemanni, Franks, Vandals, Huns, with this picture. Read the accounts by the holy men of the church, for instance, by Bishop Salvianus, of their cruelty, license, mendacity, inebriety, lust for devastation, when fate unleashed them against the unhappy Roman Empire, which, according to the accounts of Protestant theologians and ignorant Jews, was being punished for its refined enervation—and if you have an honest drop of blood in your veins you will admit that the Persians of antiquity were far superior to these protagonists of so-called reinvigoration. Herodotus marvels most in the Persians at the fact that they celebrate the anniversaries of their birthdays. In this respect, the Persians resemble the Danes, who take birthdays more seriously than any other people.

The ability of the Persians depends in high measure on that of their leader. Under the younger Cyrus, they present many fine traits, but under the king's rule, but few. They are faithless, as is shown in their treacherous attack on the generals. But any one who reads the history of Hellas through the ages, or only the history of Morea, will find the same trait recurring again and again. The Greeks, the Albanians, in fact all these races, will invite their former opponents to negotiations, offer them a banquet, and then have them treacherously cut down. Even as late as in the Italian Renaissance, in the Fifteenth and Sixteenth Centuries, we find repeated uses of this military device in times of peace. Machiavelli recognizes it as a useful method, and the Borgias did not fail to apply it.

When Cyrus inflicts the death penalty, he does so, in the *Anabasis,* after having repeatedly pardoned the traitor, and the penalty of death is carried out only after full confession has been made, as in the case where Orontas himself admits that he has been guilty of repeated acts of treason.

Cyrus then applies the death penalty with a certain elegance. Orontas is led past lines of guards who do him the customary honor of prostrating themselves before him, into a tent in which he disappears forever. We are made to understand that he is there buried alive with due dispatch.

The immeasurable superiority of the Greeks over the Persians was a physical and a spiritual superiority. The physical superiority is beyond all question. When the masses of the Persian army threatened Hellas for the first time, and when the Greeks gave evidence of a certain hesitation in giving battle against such immense numerical odds, Miltiades had a few Persian prisoners disrobed before the front, and the Greeks, their bodies nothing but muscles, trained, hardened, anointed, tanned by the sun, burst into laughter at the sight of the soft white flesh of the prisoners and immediately lost their fears.

Their spirits were not less hardened, accustomed

as they were to bear hunger, rain and cold, and sleep under the open sky. The reader will note that no one protests when Xenophon, at the beginning of the famous retreat, causes all the tents and wagons to be burned, since they cannot afford to have any camp-followers, but need every man as a combatant.

It is interesting to note the difference in the speed of Greeks and Persians in getting ready for battle. At night, says Xenophon, the Persian army is a poor army, for at night they tie their horses and attach blocks of stone to their feet. Much time is wasted in the darkness before they are seated in the saddle. Whenever the Greeks had horses, they were on their backs in an instant.

Xenophon obviously considers the Persian women to be fully as dangerous as the Persian men. He fears that if the king should permit the Hellenes to settle unmolested in the country, they would at once become enervated, and enamored of the wives and daughters of the Persians and Medeans, all of whom are pretty and shapely. As the story runs of the Lotus-eaters, the Hellenes also would soon forget to return home to their country.

A characteristic trait of the disposition of Xenophon and of his Hellenic contemporaries is that of religiosity—a religiosity amounting to a childish superstition in our eyes—consisting in the belief that the will of the gods is manifested in the nature and condition of the entrails of sacrificial beasts. But not a single Greek ever has a single doubt on this point. In this respect it might almost seem as if the Persians were superior to the Hellenes. Although Herodotus says of them that they do not believe, like the Greeks, that the gods have human forms, they give sacrifice on the tops of the highest mountains, to the entire zodiac, which means for them what Zeus means to the Greeks. In every case, they give sacrifice only to such powers as the sun, the moon, the earth, fire and water. As far as can be judged, their religiosity is far less permeated with supersition than that of the contemporary Greeks, if we ignore the Hellenic philosophers and consider only the people who, in their capacity as soldiers, were not philosophically inclined, or who, like Xenophon, were not thinkers but brave moralists.

At times, we find an ethical element in Xenophon's religiosity, as on the occasions when he strengthens the courage of his soldiers by admonishing them that heaven will punish perjury. The Persians will rue the day when they perjured themselves by murdering the Greek generals who had visited them, trusting to their plighted word, but this ethical element is exceptional. In general, the element of superstition is obvious and naïve. When Xenophon delivers his first speech to the troops concerning the dangers upon which they have embarked, and concerning the necessity of showing audacity and intelligence, a soldier happens to sneeze. Xenophon, like all the others, is delighted at this incident, and thanks Zeus for the promise of favor involved in this omen.

Day in, day out, the entrails of the sacrificial animals are used as the omens by which Xenophon determines the will of the gods. When he is chosen at Sinope to head the entire army, he declines the office, although he would like to accept it, because the auguries are unfavorable. The Laconian Cheirisofos is then elected in his place.

Xenophon offers sacrifice to all the powers that inspire him with fear. After the army has waded through the source of the Euphrates, it faces an icy blast which chills one to the bone. Xenophon offers up sacrifice to this wind, and it at once subsides.

Near the conclusion of the expedition, when the proceeds of the sale of prisoners were divided, it was determined that one-tenth of the money should be reserved as a sacrifice to Apollo and to Diana of Ephesus. Xenophon gave a portion of this money as a sacrifice to Apollo at Delphi and had his own name with that of Proxenes engraved upon the coins. The money for Diana, a large sum, was given by Xenophon to the supervisor of the temple, Megabyzes, for preservation, as Xenophon imagined he was about to face great dangers. If he should die, Megabyzes should purchase with the money the gift which in his opinion would most please Diana. When Xenophon, after his retirement, was living in the Lacedemonian city of Skillos, Megabyzes visited him and returned the sum, with which Xenophon then purchased the parcel of land traversed by the River Selenos, a name taken from another river that flowed past the famous temple of Diana at Ephesus; there he built a temple and an altar, on which he annually sacrificed to Diana one-tenth of the products of his land. This temple was a miniature counterpart of the famous Artemision, which was burned down at Herostratus two years before Xenophon's death. In return for the sacrifices brought for the goddess, Xenophon had her offer his guests who had appeared for the annual celebration he had inaugur-

wife may feel certain, on his homecoming, that no one has kissed him at the banquet (which means, no man, since only men participate in the banquets).

When Xenophon recounts the career of General Menon, he tells that Ariæos loved young men, and was therefore estranged from Menon. Menon himself was passionately in love with Tharypas, although the latter was older than he—quite an exceptional situation.

The *Anabasis* presents no cases of indignities offered to women. Cyrus had two women with him. When the Persians sacked his camp after his death, one of the women was led before the king, while the other, a Greek woman, fled naked to the Hellenes in order not to fall into the hands of the enemy. They threw a cloak about her, spared her, and took care of her, for she was young and beautiful.

In Xenophon's mind, obviously, great feminine beauty is a danger to man's peace of mind, a hindrance in the execution of his task. In the *Cyropædia,* which is a fabrication, and therefore better calculated to communicate Xenophon's own views, we read that the great Cyrus, after the victory over the Assyrians, is approached by his friend Araspes with the tidings that among the women who have been taken captive there is a young queen of Susa, of such dazzling beauty that the Persians who had entered her tent and seen her arising among her maids were thunderstruck by her beauty, her charm and elegance. They tell her that she should not bewail her fallen husband, for they will give her to a far finer man than he, to the greatest and best of men.

But Cyrus refuses not only to accept her from his men, but even to permit her to appear before him. He is afraid to lose his self-mastery. When Araspes objects that one falls in love only when one wishes it and that one can fall out of love if one prefers, since a brother of course never becomes enamored of his sister, or a father of his daughter, Cyrus answers that he has seen many persons who wished to be liberated from their infatuation as from a disease, but yet were strongly fettered by their feelings. It is true that one may not be immediately consumed in contact with fire; yet, I prefer not to come in contact with fire, and I abstain from observing a beauty.—He leaves the beautiful princess to his friend.

In the *Cyropædia* Xenophon desired to depict his ideal of a man. From the cautiousness which he ascribes to Cyrus, we may infer with some degree of plausibility that he had encountered feminine beauty at some time in his life and had not come off scot-free.

The principal charm in Xenophon is the blending of dauntless and intelligent manliness with perfect truthfulness and honor. He is an audacious man, possessed of the best culture of his time —remember he was a pupil of Socrates—and in addition he has a gift of presentation which is matchless in its simplicity.

Compare him, as a hero, with the two primitive heroes of the Hellenes, the contrasting couple Achilles and Odysseus. Achilles entirely lacks the intelligence that makes Xenophon a great leader. Odysseus, who shares his desire for adventure, entirely lacks the honorableness which makes the figure of Xenophon agreeable and not repulsive. Odysseus not only lies whenever he gets into difficulties, but he lies for the pure pleasure of it, and the auditors of the *Odyssey* admire him for this gift.

Xenophon's literary talent is shown in his characterization of the Persian and Greek generals under Cyrus. A modern parallel for Ariæos, who became a traitor at the profitable moment, is Marmont, while Masséna, with his lust for gold, parallels Menon; Clearchus, with his combination of brusqueness and condescension—as already indicated—resembles Suvarov. One morning Suvarov wakened his soldiers by his own cries of "cock-a-doodle-doo!" Clearchus has his herald shout, in order to obviate a panic: "Who let an ass loose in the camp?"

Although Clearchus has not Xenophon's culture, he is a true master in his mode of giving diplomatic replies to the Persian envoys who are sent to sound him out, answers from which they can learn nothing, and Xenophon, for his part, had the ability to restore the courage of downhearted soldiers by making circumstances that in reality were disastrous appear to be of good omen.

After the murder of the generals, the Ten Thousand were faced not only with the terrible difficulties of the terrain, and of lacking provisions, but also, they were defenseless, for they completely lacked any cavalry, while the enemy had innumerable horsemen. Xenophon fears that his troops will lose courage and become hopeless; for if they are victorious, they cannot strike down a single one of the enemies fleeing before them, and if they are defeated, not one will escape death.

He therefore explains to them that in a battle a cavalryman is really not of more account than an infantryman, for the horses cannot bite, and history presents no examples of a horse ever having brought about the death of an enemy. The foot-soldier stands firm on his own feet, while the rider can be dragged from his horse. Furthermore, the foot-soldier is far more a master of his own movements than is the horseman, who is partly at the mercy of his horse.

In this mode of reasoning, as well as in Clearchus's answers to the questions put to him, there is a trace of the logic which was the creative talent of the Greek people, a trace of the dialectics which, handed down by Socrates, are found so richly developed in Plato, and also, not a little of the sophistry which was so flourishing and fruitful among the sophists.

Very similar is the case when Xenophon is obliged to prevent his troops from losing courage when they find the country towns already burned down on their line of march, and therefore can find no forage. Xenophon interprets this situation as extremely favorable: Has not the Persian king threatened the Hellenes that he will visit their lands with fire and flame if they do not comply with his will? He must therefore be fully convinced that his cause is hopeless, since he already appears to consider Persia as the land of the Hellenes.

This merry sophistry did not fail of its effect. While generals in modern times have inflamed their soldiers with alcohol or with official bulletins —Napoleon's bulletins were fully as inflammatory as brandy—the Greek general encourages his troops with cunning sophistic reasoning of the type frequently heard by the common man from the speakers in the popular assemblies throughout Hellas.

To the honor of the little Greek mercenary army be it said that no more dauntless men can be found in the presence of an enemy of such superior numerical strength. They are so convinced of their superiority over any number of barbarians, no matter how well equipped, that they never yield an inch in any encounter, no matter how ominous their position may be.—It happens once only, toward the end of the campaign, that when a semi-savage tribe, the Mossynoikians, engaged in internecine strife with a kindred tribe that stands in the way of the Greeks, march away, they are accompanied by several scores of Greeks who join them without the permission of the generals in the hope of obtaining booty by plunder. When the Mossynoikians are defeated and run away, these Greeks run with them. The whole army feels a sense of shame that these men have taken to flight before barbarians, a thing that has never yet happened in all the campaign.

Not only do they always hold their ground, but volunteers are always ready (as in our days) for the most audacious enterprises of war, and these troops go into battle with immense good humor. Xenophon always mentions the moment when they, after the trumpet signal has been given, emit their war cry and intone the pæan. We are not told in any passage what was the text of this hymn. The important thing, after all, was the melody. Evidently it was a song of encouragement, a marching song, like the little song we have by Tyrtaios, beginning with the words:

Aget o Spartas euandru
Kuroi paterôn poliétan.

Forward now, strong Sparta's
And brave freemen's sons!
Hold firm the shield before you!
Cast forth the spear dauntless!
Spare not life and limb!
Such was never Sparta's custom.

They were aggressive, like all mercenaries, and as avaricious as hirelings always are.

Being very poor, and defenseless in their foreign environment, they were either cheated out of their pay, or the pay to which they were entitled was for long periods illegally withheld from them. Their position was particularly unfortunate after the death of Cyrus, who had recruited them, and after the beginning of their retreat without pay.

The army was as ungovernable as it was warlike. It was a miniature traveling Hellas. And Hellas was so far from being a unit that each fair-sized Greek city was wont to wage war with some other city until the latter was razed to the ground.

Even friends, when of different tribes, like the two generals Xenophon and Cheirisophos in this army, could not remain at peace with each other. Imagine this situation; they are encamped before a range of hills held by hostile troops. Xenophon says to Cheirisophos: "You Lacedemonians teach your young the art of stealing, but you flog them if they permit themselves to be caught in the act.—Now show us whether this training is of any advantage! Don't permit yourselves to be daunted in stealing these hills from the enemy, for otherwise you may expect a flogging." Cheirisophos's reply to Xenophon: "The Athenians also are said to be quite skilled in stealing, particularly from the public coffers. Show us that you have profited by your instruction! Produce some money for us!" At times the feeling between the tribes even brings about breaches of all discipline. Most of the soldiers had come from Arcadia and Achaia. In Heraklia, on one occasion, they finally hit upon the idea that it was not entirely consonant with their honor to obey an Athenian like Xenophon and a Lacedemonian like Cheirisophos. They seceded from the army and elected new leaders.

At this moment, Xenophon felt strongly tempted to leave the army, and to put out for Byzantium alone, but Herakles forbade him (by means of the entrails of a sacrificial animal) to desert the soldiers at this point.

In the last stage of its journey, the army marched in three sections, Xenophon leading only seventeen hundred hoplites and three hundred peltasts.

Meanwhile, the audacious Arcadians were faring badly. They marched ahead in order to obtain most of the booty, but were so poorly led that an entire division was cut down in Thrace. Xenophon, magnanimously overlooking the wrong they had done him, managed to relieve them in forced marches, coming upon them as they were surrounded on a hill without drinking water, and saved them from death.

What makes Xenophon's description so marvelously real is the fact that the natural conditions have remained the same to this day as they were in his. He always describes the surrounding regions with the utmost precision. Asia Minor is one of the scenes to which the oldest historical memories are attached. Homer's Asia Minor is therefore that of our day. The two springs still flow: one rather warm, the other colder—in which the Trojan women washed their shining garments. The Simois still descends from Mount Ida, "the nourisher of game, rich in springs," and unites its waters with the gentler currents of the Skamander. Field-Marshal Moltke, in his *Letters from Turkey,* reports that when he stood on a hillock, one starlight night, with the Euphrates glistening far beneath him, Xenophon's shade darted by in the moonlight. For nature is here simply stone and water, and never changes.

In 1838, Moltke made his first descent of the Euphrates on a raft of branches resting upon half a hundred inflated lamb skins that had been tied together. For this material, he says, is the only one that can be used for the purpose, since, being extremely elastic, it can bear the impact of the ceaseless collisions with the rocks in the river bed.

The reader may compare with this the passage when the Ten Thousand stand hopeless in the plain of the Euphrates, and when the men from Rhodes step forth and say: "Here are wethers, goats, oxen, and asses; flay them and blow up their hides! We shall then have 2000 such sacks, which we can tie together with the trappings of our beasts of burden and attach stones to them to serve as anchors. Then, by covering them with branches and covering the latter with dirt, so that our feet may not slip, 4000 hoplites can cross over, as over a bridge, all at the same time."—It was impossible to execute this scheme, since a numerous force of cavalry was gathering on the other bank, and it was therefore necessary to pass through the source of the Euphrates as well as that of the Tigris. But the mode of locomotion over the Euphrates seems not to have changed for more than 2,200 years.

The army waded through the source of the Euphrates with the water up to their waists. But in the hills of Armenia they were taken by surprise by a terrible snowstorm. It was necessary to wear black cloth over their eyes in order to protect them against the dazzling brightness of the snow; the cold was so great that frequently their toes were frozen. When the snow reached up to their waists—as formerly the water had—it was impossible for them to prevent themselves from freezing stiff, except by uninterrupted marching. Since their old sandals had been worn out and they had cut new ones of fresh ox-hide, the latter adhered to their feet, cutting into the flesh. Although the army was constantly pursued by numerous troops, who hurled stones and long darts at them, which penetrated both their cuirasses and their shields, the soldiers felt incapable of marching on, and lay down in the snow, exhausted, in order to sleep. This meant certain death. Xenophon went from group to group, shook the sleepers, and forced them to walk by kicking and beating them. He had to give *an example* to those who were lax and indifferent. He got up in the middle of the night, stripped himself naked, and began, in that condition, to cut wood for fuel. This gave courage to the faint-hearted. Some of them were put on horseback, the snow going up to the horses' bellies.

Xenophon's position of leader was no sinecure. Calm and objective though his presentation, far though it was from him to strike attitudes, and in spite of his fundamentally practical nature—he was not without an inherent romantic imagination. He not only hoped to enjoy in Hellas the honor of having accomplished the task of leading home ten thousand men to Hellas, through ten thousand dangers, but he dreams several times during the journey of establishing a city, of founding a colony here in Asia Minor, and of ruling it as a philosophical and literary soldier-king would do, an ambition realized some centuries later by Frederick the Great.

He first found that it would be a splendid thing to establish a city on the shores of the Pontus Euxinos (the Black Sea). But envy and calumny destroyed this plan as well as his many other projects of the same type. He of course did not wish to approach the task without first asking the gods whether they were favorable; but when he took counsel with Silanus of Arcadia, who had been soothsayer to Cyrus, the latter, who was eager to get back home in order to enjoy possession of the three thousand dareiks which he had received from Cyrus, spread the report among the Greeks that Xenophon intended to deceive the soldiers and lead them back into Asia again. Xenophon was now subjected constantly to envious calumniation. The most stupid rumors always have the confidence of the soldiers. Again and again he was forced to exclaim: "Let others take the command; I am glad to part with it."

He unmasked a certain Klearatus who had sacked a city although the generals had practically formed an alliance with this city. The soldiers went so far as to murder the messengers sent out by the city to complain of this breach of good faith.

When he made up his mind to purify the army of its vicious elements and to cause the punishment of those officers who had stolen from the war-chest, accusers rose against him on every hand. The principal accusation against him was at first that he had beaten some soldiers who had refused to get up out of the snow, in order that they might not freeze to death. Also, he had beaten a soldier whom he had ordered to carry a sick man, and whom he had surprised in the act of undertaking to bury the sick man alive in order to escape the task of carrying him.

In his reply, Xenophon expresses surprise at the fact that only the voices of those are heard whom he has (and for good reason) beaten. But none seems to recall that he helped them when they were in danger of freezing, defended them against the enemy, aided them in their trials and illnesses. No one recalls that he has been praised for a useful accomplishment or distinguished for bravery.

He dreams of cutting loose from the whole business and again plans to found a city. His enemies spread the rumor that he has bribed the soothsayer to declare the omens to be favorable. Xenophon then goes so far as to have the heralds announce that the ceremony is a public one and that anyone may be present and inspect the sacrifice while it is in progress.

Finally, the long march has obviously and completely weakened the judgment of the soldiers. When Xenophon, after the Greek army has been prevented from entering Byzantium, has explained to the soldiers the impossibility of going into combat with the Lacedemonians, who are now all-powerful throughout Hellas, a wily Theban, a certain Kyratades, an impostor, promises them that rich booty may be obtained in such an encounter. The impostor is immediately elected general, but it appears on the following day that Kyratades has not prepared provisions for the army for more than two days, and he is obliged to relinquish his post as commander.

The time had now come when the Lacedemonians planned to recruit the Ten Thousand for use in the war they were about to wage with Tissaphernes. An Arcadian arose in an assembly of the soldiers and said: "Lacedemonians! We would have joined you long ago if Xenophon had not persuaded us to come hither to Thrace, where we are hard put to it and do not receive our promised pay. I should feel that I had been fully paid if only I could be present when Xenophon is stoned to death."

Xenophon was obliged to answer, and to state that it was only for the sake of the army that he had resisted the inclination to leave it, and that he himself had not obtained the slightest fraction of the pay that had been promised him by King Seuthes.

Unselfishly he provided the troops with their pay, retaining nothing for himself, was obliged to sell his beloved horse to pay his passage to Athens, only to learn on arriving in Hellas that he had been sentenced to banishment.

This was his reward for having covered 850

parasangs, *i. e.,* 34,650 stadia, or, in the Danish language, 866 miles, in the course of 15 months, in 215 days of marching.

Posterity has given him a higher reward, but such rewards do not in the least compensate for the ingratitude of one's contemporaries.

As a writer, Xenophon later engaged in a controversy with Plato, in the *Apologia,* the *Symposion,* the *Memorabilia,* in which he was bound to be worsted. In the *Hellenika,* he reveals a certain influence of Thucydides, and in the biography of his friend, the Spartan king Agesilaos, written by Xenophon with such enthusiasm, we find traces of the influence of the orator, Isocrates.

But in the *Anabasis* he is as simple and great as a writer as he had been in his capacity of general. And in ancient Rome he was rightly regarded as a model of the unaffected charm that was termed *Atticism,* which is the same admirable quality designated to this day as *Attic salt.*

At the beginning of this account, I stated that I had been reading Xenophon at Rapallo in February. Living on this sunny coast in northern Italy, I could not become absorbed in his destinies without experiencing a desire to see his birthplace. I knew only one of the Greek islands through actually having visited it, namely, Corfu, which seems to be the island mentioned in the *Odyssey* as the fair land of the Phæacians.

And I felt a desire to stand on Attic soil, to see with my own eyes the places where Xenophon had talked with Socrates, where Plato and Aristotle taught the youth philosophy, the city from which Europe's civilization takes its origin, Athens.

HELLAS, PAST AND PRESENT

HE who has longed all his life for Attica, and who finally realizes his dream of standing on the Acropolis, is seized with a feeling of awe. For this ground is holy. These curiously tarnished marble columns, bathed in the warm, caressing March sunlight, are a festive sight to the eyes, both by their color and their form. The longer one has thirsted for this sight, the profounder is one's rapture.

It is discouraging to think that up to 1645, the Propylæa, the Erechtheion, and the Parthenon, were still practically intact. In that year, lightning struck the Propylæa, kindling the Turkish powder magazine which was sheltered by that building, with the result that this work of architectural genius was shattered. The Turks continued to make use of the Acropolis for storing their powder, now transferring the magazine to the Temple of the Parthenon. Forty-two years later, in 1687, when the Venetians were besieging Athens, one of their shells struck the Parthenon, and the most famous temple on earth was destroyed. In 1802, Lord Elgin carried off almost all of the sculptures of the Parthenon to London, where they are preserved in the British Museum, and subjected to a progressive destruction, due to the fact that they are scoured and scrubbed like the floors of the building. It would be impossible to believe this if you had not seen it with your own eyes.

Effort has been made to spread the impression that these works have been better preserved in their new domicile than would have been possible in the original climate. The proper attitude for a country at the cultural level of Great Britain would be to consider it an obvious duty to restore these stolen treasures of art to Greece.

The only advantage of their sojourn in England is in the fact that a great number of persons who can never go to Athens will have the opportunity of seeing them. But no one will prevent England from making casts of these statues. In the open air of their home they could not suffer so much from weathering as they do now owing to the moist and foggy climate of England and the vandalism to which they are exposed in that country.

Many voices have been raised in Athens in favor of permitting the Propylæa and the Parthenon to remain standing untouched, as ruins. The men who have tenderly and carefully, as well as intelligently, reërected the fallen columns, and are still tirelessly engaged in the difficult task of reassembling the sections of the columns, entirely undamaged, and of thus restoring to the temple its ancient physiognomy, have been subjected to bitter attack. However absurd restoration may be in many cases, it is here demanded by the circumstances; it is a duty to posterity. It would be wrong to permit the sections to lie scattered, when they might be made a whole by merely setting them up, without any use of cement, thus preserving the original form of the building.

And as I cast a first glance on this world of marble bathed in sunlight, on the still preserved reliefs of the Parthenon, and on the Caryatides of the Erechtheion, my inmost spirit sings: At last! At last we are no longer limited to the Dano-Greek neo-classicism of Thorvaldsen, to the Germano-Greek architecture of the Glyptothek, to the French style of La Madeline, to Greek statues as coarsened by Roman technique, to Sicilian landscapes and coastlines as a substitute for those of Greece, to the pitiable imitation known as the Athens of the North,[1] but now the true Athens, the only, eternal, true Athens!

Modern Greece does not go back farther than 1830. In 1821, the rebellion of Mavrocordato broke out against the Turks. Byron joined this movement, dying in 1824. In 1832, and again in 1824, the Turkish fleet was set on fire by the valiant Kanaris whom Victor Hugo has sung in *Les Orientales,* and whom I saw in Copenhagen with my own eyes in 1863, when this seventy-three year old man presented the Hellenic offer of the Greek throne to the prince who was later to become King George. Of all the white-bearded sages I have seen Kanaris seemed the most worthy.

In 1863, Philimon, the young secretary of the Hellenic deputation, said to me: "We hope that this little prince will one day lead us to Constantinople."—For about a century, the conquest of this city has been the national aspiration of the Greeks in present-day Hellas, a dream that is now further from its realization than ever. But the aspiration may be understood: there have always been

[1] The author probably refers to Copenhagen, although Edinburgh is sometimes also honored as "Athens of the North." —TRANSLATOR.

more Greeks in Constantinople than in Athens.

Byzantine civilization is the second product of the Greek spirit, the native Hellenic civilization being the first. The city of Byzantium lasted for more than one thousand years under that name, and it has endured for more than one thousand years more under the name of Constantinople. Byzantium was founded in the year 667 B. C., and retained that name until the year 395 A. D., a period of 1062 years, preceding the erection of the Eastern Roman Empire.

Already in 355 B. C., Byzantium had complete autonomy. Thereupon ensued the epoch of its greatest brilliancy. It fought off Philip's attack and regained its freedom after the death of Alexander the Great. The Byzantine Empire maintained itself from 395 A. D. to 1453 A. D., a period of 1058 years. If we add the epoch of Turkish rule, this city has therefore been in existence for 2589 years, for the first 2000 years of which it was entirely Greek, and later Greek at least in part.

It is, therefore, no cause for surprise that the Greeks should desire to have this city. And it is not reasonable to object—although it is perfectly true—that very few of the present inhabitants of Greece are descendants of the inhabitants of ancient Hellas. Fallmerayer pointed this out as early as 1830, but no such rigorous demand is made of any other European people. The North Germans are predominantly Slavic; the French are partly Germanic (as their very name, the *Franks,* indicates), partly Celtic, but by no means Latin, as they seem to think.

It is possible that an excessively large proportion of Albanian and Slavic blood flows in the veins of the present-day Greeks; yet they are descended from the Greeks of antiquity; and memory, tradition, particularly their language, which is still written with the characters used three thousand years ago, makes them feel themselves to be the sons and daughters of Hellas.

They are so keen on the subject of their ancient written language, that they even rose against Queen Olga, a Russian woman, in a well-known insurrection, when the Queen—with the best of all intentions—had caused the New Testament to be translated and printed in the Greek vernacular as actually spoken. While the Norwegians may hold their national language very dear, surely the Greeks do not hold theirs less so.

During the tension of the World War, the first misfortune of Greece was due to the fact that King

Constantine was married to a sister of William II. But honor is also due to the English, French, and Italian pseudo-statesmen for the storms of misfortune that have crushed Greece to earth.

In the year 1881, Hellas, after having remained neutral during the Russo-Turkish War, obtained possession of Thessaly and Southern Epirus, which was one of the provisions of the Congress of Berlin.

Crete was still under Turkish domination. When the island rose in rebellion for the second time, in 1896, the Greek Government could no longer ignore the influence of the Greater Greece movement and occupied Crete in 1897. After a disgraceful defeat at the hands of the Turkish army, the Greeks had to evacuate Thessaly, but were permitted to retain this territory by paying an enormous indemnity.

A military insurrection in 1910 brought the energetic and unscrupulous Venizelos to the helm. His psychology was determined by the fact that, being a Cretan, he considered all Turks to be enemies entitled to no quarter.

The First Balkan War against Turkey, in which King Constantine—then not yet king—made his reputation as a general, gained Southern Macedonia, Saloniki, Janina, for Greece. During his triumphal entrance into the city of Saloniki, which is not Greek, but inhabited by Jews who speak Spanish, King George was murdered, in March, 1913, by a madman.

After the Second Balkan War, in which (July, 1913) the enemy was Greece's former ally, Bulgaria, Greece was considerably enlarged, obtaining Crete, the whole of Epirus, and—in 1916—southern Albania in addition.

When the World War broke out, Hellas at first declared itself neutral. But, owing to his German queen, King Constantine was suspected by the Western powers of German sympathies, although no one thought of impugning the King of Denmark, or the King of Belgium, for the German origin of their wives. The Entente coöperated with Venizelos to oppose him. When the King replaced Venizelos in 1915 by Gunaris, a rival government was erected in Saloniki, and the powers treated Venizelos as an ally, as the true representative of Greece. In June, 1917, Venizelos, at the head of French Negro troops, marched into Athens and had machine guns set up on the Square of the Constitution, the center of the city. On the instigation of the national police authorities, who had assumed power, the grove surrounding the country seat of Tatoi, in which the King[1] lived, was set on fire in four different quarters, as a witness, a Greek Minister, assures me. The entire park, as well as the palace, was destroyed by the flames, leaving only a few stumps and the rocky ground, and the King, having been smoked out, was obliged to abdicate. Censored telegrams recorded that the palace had been set on fire by a short circuit. The Allies, who had no confidence in the Crown Prince—the present King—a four-square young man of energetic features, made the youngest son, Alexander, King. The French occupied the Piræus. When the aroused population shot down about a dozen marines, the anger of the military occupation authorities, of course, increased.

Venizelos assumed control, whereupon Hellas carried out the Allied order to declare war against Germany and Austria, Bulgaria and Turkey.

The Greeks, to be sure, were not in a position to inflict any particular damage on any of the Central Powers, and besides, they had had their fill

[1] Constantine, who abdicated on Sept. 27, 1922, died at Palermo, on January 11, 1923.—TRANSLATOR.

[2] Greece was proclaimed a republic on March, 25, 1924; King George II, the "present" king, above mentioned, had escaped to Rumania with his queen (Elizabeth) a few days before the republic was proclaimed.—TRANSLATOR.

in the Balkan Wars. But France needed the Greek troops for other purposes. France had Venizelos send a Greek division to the assistance of Denikin, the general who fought with so little success in the Ukraine against the Soviet Government, in 1919. But few of these Hellenes remained alive to tell the tale. The poor wretches laid down their lives for a cause that did not inspire them, that did not in fact concern them at all, and which they could not even understand. What had they to do with the form of government in Russia! But the Powers did not fail to find a new function for the Greek army. During the Peace Conference in Paris, Orlando made it perfectly plain that Italy considered herself as badly treated by her allies. Presumably, Italy's share of the loot had been too small. And, by virtue of a secret treaty with England and France, Italy demanded the right to land her troops in Smyrna.

Now it transpired that neither Clemenceau, nor Lloyd George, nor Wilson, had any desire to see an Italian army in Asia Minor.

Furthermore, it appeared that England did not trust France, nor—for that matter—did France trust England, sufficiently for either country to permit the other to gain a firm foothold in Smyrna or the environment.

In casting about, their eyes hit upon Greece as the natural rival of Italy. Of course, Venizelos lent a hand, and, sadly enough, the first troops he forwarded were the remnants of the Greek division which he had once placed at the disposal of General Denikin. In the official report issued by the Allies on May 15, 1919, we read that these troops "were sent out to prevent any attack by the Turks on the Christian population."

No one with a heart in his breast can now hear the name "Smyrna" without having that heart bleed.

The many young girl students in the University of Athens in the spring of this year, vivacious, sensible young girls, almost all came from Smyrna. And when asked how their lives had been since childhood under Turkish rule, they declared—but without complaint—that they had grown up in constant danger: "Since our earliest childhood we were accustomed, at the cry: *The Turks are coming!,* to rush into cellars and keep as still as mice until they were gone again. Then we would again venture out and look around to see whether the danger was past; a few corpses would be lying in the streets in their own blood; in our childlike thoughtlessness we soon forgot about the incident."

In May, 1919, the Greeks occupied Thrace. They also landed in Smyrna, took possession of the city, and pressed forward to the interior of Asia Minor. It seems that the Greek army, whose hostility to the Turks is rather religious than national in character, was not guilty of any such atrocities. The Turks maintained that the Greeks set villages on fire; this is not improbable—man at war is always a wild animal—but the accusation is, of course, made in order to justify the cruelties of the Turks, which are an hundred-fold worse.

At the San Remo Conference, Venizelos was selected by the Allies for the purpose of forcing the Allied Peace Treaty upon Turkey. In return, the Sèvres Treaty was to assure Greece a further enlargement of territory. The Allies commissioned the Greeks to rob provinces from Turkey; probably because they believed Greece to be incapable of executing this task or rather, perhaps, because they imagined they might thus—without running any risk themselves—punish Turkey severely for having allied itself with Germany.

While Venizelos in the eyes of the Allies was the chosen national hero of all the Greeks, and had indeed been quite instrumental in enabling this little country to achieve a fairly powerful position, he had sacrificed most of his popularity in his own country. His harshness had been repellent and had aroused serious opposition: he exiled the royal family to Switzerland, threw ministers like Royos into jail for indefinite periods—three years in the case of Royos—had the whole court carried off, distinguished gentlemen and delicate ladies, who have themselves told me about it, handed over to the French authorities, and incarcerated, together with Gunaris, a minister hated by Venizelos, in a little Corsican hotel, where they were held in captivity and had to account daily for every franc they spent. This Corsican captivity lasted for two and one-half years.

One day Gunaris seized an opportunity to escape to Sardinia with a young courtier, his assistant. Thereupon, the other gentlemen and ladies of the court were treated with even greater severity. They were considered as accessories to the flight of Gunaris, of which they were not guilty. But of course it would have been contrary to their conception of honor to betray their fellow-countrymen. They simply waited until the discovery was made, some days later, that Gunaris was gone.

Therefore, there was considerable dissatisfaction with Venizelos among the Greek population, even though he had—and still has—a great number of devoted and enthusiastic supporters. No one doubts his ability.

King Alexander died suddenly, of the bite of a little monkey, in October 1920.—On November 14, 1920, Venizelos was deposed from his position as dictator, by a general election, and in the following month, namely, December, King Constantine was recalled to Athens by popular vote. If Venizelos had been ruthless against the king's adherents, the king's adherents were now ruthless against the Venizelists. Admiral Konduriotis was shot down in his parlor by hired bandits, who on the same occasion shot an amiable lady, with whom I am acquainted, and who happened to be sitting in the room at the time, in the shoulder. Attacks from ambuscade in streets and squares were the regular order of the day in the month of March. The murderers were never discovered.

King Constantine is a tall, upright man of stubborn character. His position in the years 1921–22 was extremely delicate. Whenever he went to the Piræus, the English and French ships lying in port would make for the open sea, in order to avoid the necessity of saluting him. Neither the English nor the French, nor the United States minister would greet the King on meeting him in the street, at a concert, or in any other public place. They would salute his ministers and do business with them, but not the King. The King had constructed the curious theory that he could get along without the recognition of the Powers. This may be explained only by the fact—which I have from the best authority—that England's relations with him were nevertheless secretly friendly. Furthermore, he maintained that the recognition and devotion of his people were sufficient for him. Yet his people, after he had been again exiled, left him in the lurch; they were faithful only during his period of good fortune. For he did have such a period. The fortunes of war were favorable to the army in Anatolia. For a year it marched from victory to victory. It conquered a territory of 116,000 square kilometers, including the only railroad in the country, and was about to take Angora, after a victory in the bloodiest battle in the war.

It was not the King who had undertaken this war in Asia Minor; it was Venizelos. For three years, the war had been going on. It had cost three hundred million dollars and an enormous number of human lives. It seemed ridiculous to relinquish what had been gained, and yet it also seemed absurd to continue the war. For, while the latter had been started on the instigation of the Western Powers, those Powers were not favorably impressed with its progress. European capitalists were not glad to see the Greeks own a spacious and fruitful area, to whose treasuries the great bankers under Turkish rule had had very easy access. Italy did not wish to tolerate a powerful Hellas, with a large fleet in the Eastern Mediterranean; France could not bear to think of British hegemony in Asia Minor, and considered Greece to be merely a pawn in the hands of England. Neither victorious Serbia nor conquered Bulgaria looked with favorable eyes on a rising Hellas, especially since it was possible that Hellas might not stop in its course before reaching Constantinople.

Therefore, France suddenly changed her attitude on Turkey. When allied with Germany, the French ambition was to cut Turkey to pieces. In French newspapers, this country had been a barbarous power, whose European possessions must all be taken away without exception. But of course, this view changed as soon as Turkey was no longer the old Turkey, but a new Turkey. In November, 1916, Aristide Briand had branded the outrageous cruelties of the Young Turks in the most emphatic language. In January, 1917, he again spoke of the necessity of freeing the nations from the bloody tyranny of the Turks. In the year 1920, he was still speaking of the nations moaning under the Turkish yoke. But in 1921, he affixed his signature to the Angora Agreement. For now Turkey had become a power that might be used against England, against English Imperialism, or against Greek Imperialism, which was considered a sort of cryptoform of the English prototype. For it was clear that the English in Asia Minor would fight to the last—Greek.

Fortunately for the Turks, they also had found their Venizelos, a brave, ruthless gentleman who, when still a colonel, had stormed the English redoubts at Gallipoli, a statesman who had already entered into close contact with Soviet Russia. As early as October, 1918, Trotsky had wisely established a Mohammedan Military Academy at Kazan. In December, 1919, there came Kemal's declaration to the effect that he and the Bolsheviki had interests in common.

France, in her political arrogance, had mortally offended Russia, had equipped against her the Czecho-Slovaks, Kolchak, Denikin, Wrangel, and the Poles. The intelligent and amiable Edouard Herriot, my good friend, had to start for Moscow at once.

Mustapha Kemal was the man of the moment, and he became France's man too. The French factories furnished Kemal with cargo after cargo of artillery, particularly with the famous 75 mm. field guns, and French aëroplanes. Colonel Mougin, former chief of staff of General Gouraud, proceeded to Angora, in order to discuss economic questions with Kemal. In spite of England's passionate protests, the French and Italians stubbornly refused to permit the Greeks to visit and search the ships bringing guns and ammunition to the Turks.—Hardly a month had passed since Lloyd George had declared in the Lower House: "We cannot permit this thing to go on forever," namely, permit the Turks to scorn English proposals, permit England's allies to refuse Greece the right to make use of her military power in order to occupy Constantinople. For the Greeks had turned down the Allied demand that they evacuate Asia Minor and resolved to terminate the war with a bold offensive against Constantinople.

But the Allies convoked a conference at Venice in order to determine under what circumstances the Greeks should leave Asia Minor. The Greek Government itself understood how weak was its position, and after no less than ten years of war, the fighting spirits of their soldiers were exhausted. The drachma was not worth a penny; the daily provisioning of the troops had become impossible. Mustapha Kemal was speedily informed of the extreme weakness of the Greek front at Afium Kara Hissar, and splendidly equipped with a generous supply of French 75's, and with French and Italian aëroplanes, with trucks and lorries of the latest construction, and also with a staff of able French officers, he fell upon the Hellenic army with destructive force, at a moment when the Greeks had been tied hand and foot by their own allies, who had refused to prevent the enemy from receiving imports of war materials.

The result was the most disastrous defeat in the history of Greece. The entire army was destroyed in its flight to Smyrna.

In the harbor at Smyrna, English, French,

American and Italian ships of war lay at anchor; the Christian inhabitants of the city therefore had misgivings. There lay before them these invincible destroyers, these massive battleships, ready to defend them. But they fired not a shot. France had already proposed that it have free rein on the Rhine, while England should dispose of Asia Minor. England had not consented and would not consent to this proposal, for a further seizure of German soil could only have substituted military control by France over the Continent, for the pre-war military control of the Continent by Germany. As a result, the French took revenge on England by permitting the Turks, who had recently been the common enemy, to destroy unmolested the Greek people who were being goaded on and utilized as a pawn by England.—The key to all these happenings is the silent struggle between France and England, the harbinger of the next war.

Frightful events had preceded the cutting down and burning up of the population of Smyrna, together with the conflagration of the entire Christian quarter of the city.

It was not without cause that Smyrna had been filled with hundreds of thousands of fugitives. As early as in the summer of 1915, the German ambassador to Turkey, Count Wolf-Metternich, wrote to Bethmann-Hollweg, who was then chancellor: "No one can any longer hold back the chauvinism and fanaticism of the Turks. The Committee no longer means merely an organized government party at Constantinople, but now extends its authority over every vilayet. The banishment of the Armenians is already begun; their property has everywhere been confiscated. If an Armenian owned a house valued at, let us say, 100, it is allotted to some Turk, some member or friend of the Committee, at the price of 2. But," Wolf-Metternich continued, "the pack of hounds is already impatiently preparing for the moment when Greece, egged on by the Entente, will turn against Turkey. Then there will be a mass-murder far exceeding that of the Armenians. The victims are more numerous, the booty far more enticing. For Hellenism is the cultural element in Turkey."

Even before the World War (according to the reasonable estimate made by that great and good man, Dr. Lepsius), 727,000 Greeks were driven out of their domiciles in May and June of 1914, and forced to take refuge on the islands or in Hellas. During the era of persecutions, in 1915–16, the Turks had murdered 240,000 Greeks in the interior of Asia Minor. This may not seem a large number as compared with the number of Armenians murdered in the same period, which was 1,200,000, to which we must add the 300,000 who fled to the Caucasus. But, according to Greek and American reports, which are in perfect agreement, this figure of one and a half millions of Armenians gradually (even before the Græco-Turkish War) was increased by a full million of Greeks and Syrians, so that altogether Turkey got rid of 2,500,000 Christians in this manner.

From May, 1921 to January, 1923, according to the authoritative statement of Dr. Mark Ward, the American director of the hospital at Kharput, 20,378 persons, of whom 18,000 were Osmanli Greeks and 2,000 Armenians, were deported, *i. e.,* driven out to die of starvation and cold. And as soon as the mountain roads became passable this spring, new transports—those still surviving—passed through Kharput. All these, men, women, and children, knew that they were being driven forth to die. All the Turkish officials knew it as well. There was no possibility of finding shelter or food in these bare hills.

All these things had gone on behind Kemal's front. Now came Kemal himself with his infuriated bands. When the population in Smyrna became aware that they were threatened, they fled to the Quay, in order to call upon their protectors. But not even the women, who cast off their clothing and swam out to the warships, were received on board; for that a passport would be required. Then the city was sacked, men killed by the thousands, women violated by the thousands. In the American home for fatherless and motherless children alone, three hundred little children were burned alive. Females of the age of ten and older were not only violated but tortured and passed on from one bestial persecutor to the other. Their breasts were cut off, their eyes gouged out, their stomachs cut open.

The only government that acted honorably and decently on this occasion was the Greek Government, which sent out every available ship to help, as well as nurses from the Greek army. The government kept public kitchens going as long as it was possible.

But now the city of Athens, a small and poor capital of 300,000 inhabitants, a city about to enter the stage of expansion, has become the asylum for more than half a million fugitives from Asia Minor—some persons say as many as 750,000—and it is impossible to afford them all shelter and nourishment. Most of them are women and children, deprived of every necessity.—For the Western Powers have more than 200,000,000 Mohammedan subjects who must not be irritated.

In his famous prayer on the Acropolis, a classic bit of prose, Ernest Renan expressed among other things the hope that all the nations that have appropriated statues and fragments of these temples might reach so high a stage of culture as to give them back. But the matter now is far more serious.

It is a far cry from the feelings expressed by Renan in his prayer, to those now animating the European Powers in their relations with Hellas. These Powers have sacrificed Hellas to the fury of the Turks in cold blood. Greece, not Palestine, is the Holy Land, and until humanity recognizes this fact, until humanity discards its indifference to truth and its hatred for reason, which in our day is cankering all souls and permeating all of literature and philosophy, we shall witness nothing more nor less than a continuous and progressive decay of our civilization.

I am, of course, aware that the Hellas of antiquity was by no means an ideal state. I know very well that deep-seated envy, parading as morality, and a hatred of greatness, are among the fundamental passions of man, and were therefore epidemic even in ancient Hellas.

Miltiades, victor at Marathon, died in prison.

Themistocles, victor at Salamis, was banished and obliged to flee to the Persians.

Pericles, the greatest statesman of Athens, was sentenced to pay an enormous fine and had to relinquish all his offices.

Anaxagoras, the greatest thinker of his day, fled, accused of blasphemy, and was sentenced to death, *in contumaciam.*

Aspasia, the most famous woman of ancient Greece, accused of blasphemy and immorality, escaped the death penalty only because Pericles begged in tears for her life.

Socrates, the greatest philosopher of Greece, was condemned to die by drinking poison.

Alcibiades, the most resplendent figure in ancient Hellas, a general of extraordinary gifts, was condemned to death for his so-called blasphemy, banished, and then recalled. In his capacity as an Athenian general, he defeated the Spartans, who finally had him murdered in Persia. One human creature only, an *hetaira,* remained faithful to him.

Plato, the greatest prose writer of ancient Greece, the most renowned creative thinker even to our own day, was treated as a prisoner of war by Dionysios in Sicily and sold as a slave to Ægina.

Xenophon, like Plato a disciple of Socrates, a wandering knight, who saved the lives of the Ten Thousand, was banished from Athens as a friend of Sparta, and deprived of his property.

Aristotle, antiquity's most noted philosopher, the teacher of Alexander the Great, had to flee from Athens under the accusation of being a friend of the Macedonians, and died on the island of Eubœa.

Phidias, the most famous sculptor that ever lived, was accused first of theft, then of sacrilege, finally of burglary, and, a sick man, terribly depressed, died in prison.

Demosthenes, the most famous orator of Greece as well as of the world in general, was thrown into prison, later escaping to Ægina. After having been recalled and sentenced to death by the Macedonian party, he escaped to a temple and took poison in order to escape arrest.

The glorious image of the ancient Hellas that

is sacred to me is, therefore, not without its dark spots. And yet—what light!

He whose eyes have been opened to the revelation involved in Hellenic activity cannot possibly stand on the Acropolis without beholding the temples again rising before his eyes in all their former grandeur. The Acropolis is the pedestal for the fairest buildings that have risen from the earth. What a stirring spectacle is presented to the eyes of him who stands in the Theater of Dionysos, so miraculously preserved at the foot of the cliff, where to this day you may still clearly read under the marble seats for whom the best places were reserved; for the highest officials of the town, the archons and judges. Every character may still be read with perfect clearness. A shudder of holy awe fills one's soul at the thought that it was this stage that bore the performances of the precious works of Euripides and his enemy Aristophanes, while the Athenians were following the performance breathlessly, their eyes and ears wide open.

The uncanny cave not far away, which was truly a place of captivity, and a dreadful one at that, can hardly have been the place in which Socrates drank his cup of hemlock, although it bears that name. If this was the place, Plato's descriptions in the *Kriton* and the *Phaido* are all wrong. The interior of this prison is frightfully dark. Yet it is possible that Plato, who was not present either when Socrates delivered his speech in his own defense, but rewrote it from his own impressions, was also absent from the cell in which Socrates was imprisoned, and therefore did not behold the latter in captivity and could not know what were the circumstances of his incarceration. I personally, however, cannot believe that Socrates could have maintained his spiritual equilibrium to the end, as he did, if he had been imprisoned in this dark and gloomy hole.

Another monument of antiquity, not far from here, is no doubt quite genuine: namely, the cliff of the Areopagus, on which the highest court had its seat. It still stands, precipitous and inaccessible, with all the dignity of the memories connected with it since Æschylus wrote his *Oresteia*. And yet, it is quite probable that as many unrighteous as righteous judgments were spoken on its summit. Justice has ever been an ideal merely.

The Athens Museum affords a general view of the evolution of Greek sculpture since the days of Solon, when the body of a serpent was depicted in the tympanum of the Hekatompedon (made of the soft stone known as *poros*) with three torsos bearing bearded heads with a smile of archaic outlines, down to the period that presents an ever-increasing mastery in the treatment of the Pentelic marble.

The oldest work in marble, the Calf-Bearer, is doubtless the model for the many primitive Christian representations of the Good Shepherd with the Lamb on his shoulder.

The many statues of Athene and of the young girls who were called *Kore* by the Greeks, are all austere, fully clothed and treated with a seriousness that knows no smile.

This great art culminates in the wonderful relief of the Goddess of Victory, *Nike,* who is tying her sandals in order to rush to the battlefield.—Borne aloft by the beat of her wings, and touching earth but for a moment, the goddess bends over to tie her sandals, then to dart on as a bird. This figure is a matchless study in drapery. The faultless body is visible through the numerous folds of the transparent material of her garment.

This relief is taken from the Bastion of Kimon on the Acropolis, where the temple of the wingless Pallas Athene once stood. Only after the victory of the Greeks over the Persians did she receive the name of *Nike.* The relief was a portion of the frieze representing the battle at Platæa in the year 479 B. C.

The statue itself was executed about 410 B. C.

The west side of the frieze of the Parthenon was a representation of the procession in the Pan-Athenaic festival. The most aristocratic young girls of the city are delivering to the goddess the veil which they themselves have woven; they are accompanied by the handsomest young men, who are on horseback.

Among the reliefs preserved on the Acropolis, that of the mounted youth with the bowed head and the broad hat is extremely expressive and unforgettable. It was on this figure that Victor Cherbuliez wrote his youthful work, *Un cheval de Phidias.*

Truly these horses are hardly less entrancing—though less Greek—than the youths themselves. Phidias took his models for these horses from the lightest breed of horses known, namely, the Arab horses, which in those times were already supplied to Hellas. He conventionalized these horses, relieved them of all their trappings, of saddle and harness, clipped their manes, causing them to stand on end, and therefore not concealing the outlines of the horse's neck as they would if permitted to descend. The lightness of the horses is matched by the relaxation evident in the composed walk of the virgins, the supple forms of the young horsemen, the simple motions of the hands and the clear eyes of the old men, the gentle flowing motion of all the garments. The procession in marble extended for 530 feet (160 meters) and yet did not seem too long.

The reader will permit me to mention, before I close, a visit made by me to the plains of Marathon, in splendid weather, which permitted me to enjoy the rich vegetation, the olive trees, the fields of asphodel, the abundance of blossoms at a season when snow is lying on the ground in our country. It is a moving moment for the admirer of Greece, when he regards the spot where the hundred thousand Persians stood, when he sees the protection afforded to the army after its landing, and when he knows where the thousand horsemen of the Persians halted, while the Greek hoplites, without any cavalry at all, only 10,000 men altogether, stood to oppose them one to ten. I am not counting the armor bearers, of whom each man of both the opposing armies had one for himself. You can trace the strategy of Miltiades on this battlefield; his aim was to keep his wings strongest, in order, when his center should yield to the advance of the Persians, to fall upon the enemy's flank. You may sit for hours on the still existing funeral mound, Tymbus, under which the charred remnants of the 195 fallen Hellenes have been found, and you may there enjoy the breakfast you have brought with you, and lose yourself in thought.

The battles that later attained world-historic importance, for the reason that they determined the destinies of civilization, were then fortunately not so bloody as in our days, when men fall by tens of thousands, and in which in reality nothing is decided except a retrogression of civilization along the path of destruction.

You may travel from Athens to Eleusis by carriage, along the Bay of Salamis—of glorious memory! Your journey passes over the sacred road of antiquity, near the much-sung olive groves, past the little Byzantine monastery of Daphni, whose mosaics resemble those of Ravenna, to the ruins of the Eleusynian mysteries, standing on a cliff. These mysteries were a sort of free-masonry; they consisted of dramatic presentations of mysterious symbols from the life of Demeter and Persephone, symbols of the sowing of the grain in the earth and of the growth of the grain: death and resur-

pose any exceptional exertions on his voice, and then, further down, the entire city spread out just as it was twenty-five hundred years ago. At last I was able to stand on the spot from which Demosthenes had spoken, and I recalled his speeches, particularly the short speech defending the young officers who had been guilty of excessive drinking in a garrison town and had then disturbed the peace in the streets of the town. This speech is a vivid reflection of every-day life in ancient Greece.

Demosthenes was an impassioned, at times an injudicious, at times even a fanatical man, by no means a saint. He was a great orator in the latter days of free Hellas, greater even than his opponent Æschines, although the latter was a close second. But he was an exceptionally brave man, as brave as he was eloquent. It is unfortunate that he should have had among his opponents such men as Philip of Macedon and Alexander the Great. He did not understand what a great thing it would have been if all those who spoke Greek could have been united into a single nation, regardless of whether they had been born in Macedonia, in Attica, or in the Peloponnesus. His love of freedom blinded his eyes to the fact that unity was more important for the small states than liberty.

In his day, he could still see from Pnyx the Acropolis with its Parthenon undamaged, and with all the holy places that drew one's thoughts to Pallas Athene.

Athene was the daughter of Zeus, who had sprung from his brow, which is the sunlit sky. No mother bore her. She was the purity of the radiant air; the air's virgin whiteness, with its engaging and awe-inspiring influence. About her was the invigorating briskness of the atmosphere when it has been purified by thunder and storm. Her eyes were of the blue of the sky.

Her cataclysmic birth had made her war-like, armed cap-a-pie, formidable. Her birth, which had proceeded to the accompaniment of thunder and lightning, was not without its effect. No Hellene could ever imagine her as an old maiden lady. She was Thought itself; ultimately she became also spirit and reason. She invented the arts; she tamed the horse. To her the Athenians owed the delicate ingenuity of their spirit. Being the incarnation of thought in action, she had the majesty of the eternal. As I said last year: "A Northern race, obtaining its religion from a German monk who substituted the Bible for the Pope, and then engaged in hand-to-hand combat with

It is not impossible that Plato may have fallen into the former extreme, that of misanthropy. But he was too Greek at bottom to become a victim to the other extreme, that of a hatred of reason.

Life remains perpetually the same entrancing and depressing tragedy that was once played in the Theater of Dionysos. We are obliged to act our part in the play. All a man can do is to exert every effort to choose his rôle correctly, to choose whether he will be a scoundrel, a fool, a coward, or a man.

THE COLLAPSE OF GREECE

IF any specific European diplomat may be mentioned as responsible for the collapse that has brought Hellas to its present low estate, that man could be none other than Lord Grey, for he it was who, as early as 1915, struck upon the idea of utilizing Venizelos for the purpose of splitting the Greek people and generating the fanatical party spirit which has divided the families of Athens, even brothers and sisters, into hostile camps producing one atrocity and assassination after the other, until the entire situation culminated in a massacre of all the country's official ministers, as well as the general-in-chief of the army, in a judicial mass-murder.

Of all the birds of ill omen that were beating about with their wings during the World War, Lord Grey is one of the most unpleasant specimens. He lied again and again to the Parliament of his country; he kept his evil plans hidden from his own colleagues in the Cabinet. He has a brand upon his brow.

The events of the last quarter of a year in Greece are still unexplained. They are as unclear as the origin of the World War would still be if the Soviet Government had not, on attaining power, published the entire correspondence of Izvolsky, a veritable wagon-load of secret documents.[1]

But the events in Greece are so recent, and the frantic efforts to make what has happened remain inscrutable are so powerful and so stubborn, that it is difficult to obtain a complete account anywhere.

Let us begin at the beginning: Who started the revolution of September 26?[2] By whose permission and on whose command did the Greek fleet put to sea from Constantinople, transporting rebellious troops to Athens, who there were to overthrow the Constitution? Who instructed these rebellious soldiers to take up their position in front of the French Legation and shout hurrahs for France on the day of their arrival in Athens? Why could the English Minister, who protected Gunaris and his associates from murder on September 28, not protect them precisely two months thereafter?

[1] Translations of these secret treaties between various Allied Powers, including Russia, were first published in America by the *New York Post* in January, 1918.—TRANSLATOR.

[2] 1922.—TRANSLATOR.

We do not know the answers to these questions, which are kept carefully concealed from us. The motives are secret, as all motives have been kept secret in this century, in which the various powers that be have been governed—not unreasonably—by the principle that *the public do not think.* If the public should ever undertake to ask questions, they are pacified by means of more or less plausible cut-and-dried answers.

The few persons capable of thought have not much opportunity to make themselves heard in our day, and if they speak the truth, it is easy to render them suspicious and thus silence them. The thing that we used to term simply a lie in the old days, and which is now more justly designated as politics, is an organized power.

Now and then something may leak out, something that appears to serve as a light or a guide. But soon thereafter the weakness and vacillation of men's characters again set in, making it impossible to gain any information as to what has really been going on.

In May, 1920, Lloyd George informed Venizelos that the latter could no longer count on support from France or Italy, or even England, since unfortunately even the British Secretary for Foreign Affairs was a friend of Turkey. But he declared, nevertheless, that his own attitude was favorable to the Hellenic cause.

And we find that in February, 1921, he asked Constantine's representative at the London Conference whether the Greek Government considered itself strong enough to defeat Kemal's army. As he obtained an affirmative answer, he declared himself to be entirely on the side of Greece, and when the Greek offensive in Asia Minor seemed, at its outset, to be meeting with success, his secretaries telephoned twice every day to the Greek Legation in London, and Lloyd George himself made no attempt to conceal his delight.

The negotiations with the Greek delegation were not conducted by the Secretary for Foreign Affairs, but by the Prime Minister, Lloyd George, himself, and it was Lloyd George himself who hinted to the Greeks that the different proposals based on the revision of the Sèvres Treaty, which were favorable to Turkey, might be calmly rejected by Greece, so long as Greece was able to bring the war in Asia Minor to a victorious conclusion, and this, he said, would be the best solution for Great Britain and for Hellas.

When the Greeks resumed hostilities, it was for

the reason, therefore, that they had been assured of England's sympathy, and that they had faith in their own warlike prowess. Since, for a long time after the start of the war, it seemed that the Greeks would win—they were victorious in the Battle of Eski Shehir in July, 1921—Lloyd George declared publicly that Greece was now entitled to obtain more than was allowed it by the Sèvres Treaty.

But when things began to go wrong, it did not occur to Lloyd George to support his hard-beset friends, but he informed Gunaris that Constantine's return—in spite of the fact that he had been called back to Greece by ninety-eight per cent. of the Greek people—made it impossible for the Allies to support Greece any longer. Therefore, Lloyd George was now fighting for the freedom of the Straits, or whatever you may call it (as he had once fought to make the world safe for democracy). Shortly thereafter, he disappeared through a trap-door and was gone forever.

But the double game continued. I have mentioned above (page 184) the remarkable fact that at the same time when the English minister in Athens was officially and demonstratively neglecting to salute the King, the King himself was declaring that the relations between his Government and that of Great Britain were all that could be desired. And the speech of Prime Minister Demetrius Gunaris before the Council of War confirms the King's statement. Gunaris spoke on the day before he was attacked by the typhus. He knew that his life was forfeited; he spoke to defend his honor. And he said: "My actions are justified by the fact that I had received secret, but none the less official, encouragement from the British Government, in the form of a written promise, signed by Lord Curzon himself."

England's friendship for Greece was, as the events have shown, a conditional and hypothetical friendship. The English Minister in Athens did not prevent a little band of rebellious officers, none having higher rank than that of a colonel, from shooting down six of the most trustworthy men in Greece, including three former prime ministers, without trial or sentence, but he protested against this action by leaving Athens, returning again a few days later, as soon as he had had an opportunity to make his report to Lord Curzon at Lausanne. He does not seem to have dared leave the French Legation alone on the ground in Athens, nor did he prevent King Constantine from being banished; but he saw to it that the King suffered no indignities, put him under the protection of an English Admiral, and gave him £5,000 traveling money. Time was when England's attitude was more manful, when England's wrath was more feared, and England's assistance more valuable.

At any point at which you study the question, you always find England giving Greece the most absurd and useless advice. Never do England's words seemed backed by a man.

In January, 1922, at the Cannes Conference, both Lloyd George and Lord Curzon outlined to Gunaris the peace plan which they proposed to submit in Paris. But this peace plan was postponed, and in February, Gunaris wrote to Lord Curzon that the Greek army could not possibly hold out any longer in Asia Minor unless it immediately obtained munitions and money from England.

Lord Curzon took his time about replying, not sending his answer before March 6, and then expressing only the incredibly stupid thought that the position did not seem so critical to him as to Gunaris, and that he hoped that the Greek army would turn out to be the equal of Turkey's army. He advised Gunaris to wait for the advice of the Allies after their meeting, which was to take place at an early date. Fearing to displease England, the unhappy Gunaris was obliged to yield and content himself with this absurd declaration.

Thereupon the Allies, after their Paris meeting, issued a proposal of peace that was accepted by Greece. Turkey, however, rejected the proposal, and the Allies—for excellent reasons—made no attempt to oblige Turkey to acquiesce, since both France and Italy had all they could do to supply the Turks with cannons and munitions, for the purpose of injuring Hellas, which was England's protégé, and through Hellas, England itself, their beloved companion in arms.

On July 18, Lloyd George asked the Greeks if they could hold out for another winter in Asia Minor. When the Greeks replied that it was possible they might be able to do so, but only on the condition that money and munitions should immediately be furnished by England, he sent them nothing, but delivered so encouraging a speech about the Greeks in Parliament on November 4, that this speech was issued to the Greek Army as an order of the day.

When, immediately before the collapse, the Greek Government addressed a final desperate appeal to Lloyd George, merely entreating him to bring about an armistice with all possible speed, in order to enable the army to evacuate Asia Minor immediately, he answered, with paternal superiority, with the admonition that the Greeks should not, in the panic of the moment, forget their dignity and accept conditions that would humiliate them: they should calmly go ahead and take up the battle with the Turks outside of Smyrna. It seemed incredible to him that they should not be able to stop the Turkish army.

Then followed the frightful defeat which the Greek Government had done everything in its power to prevent, and which the two "incredulous" English statesmen, Lloyd George and Lord Curzon, had done their best to bring about.

In August, 1922, the Turks, equipped with French cannons and Italian aëroplanes, fell upon the Greek army at Afium-Kara-Hissar and annihilated it. On September 26—it is not known by whose order—rebellious Greek troops were transported from Constantinople to Athens.

On November 28, Demetrius Gunaris, now for the third time Prime Minister, and for the seventh time Minister, leader of the constitutional People's Party in the National Assembly that was elected on November 14, 1920; Nikolas Stratos, former Prime Minister and leader of the Reform Party; Georgios Baltadjis Protopapadakis, former Prime Minister, and on several occasions Minister of Finance; Nikolas Theotokis, former Greek Minister to Berlin, later Commander-in-chief of the Greek troops in Asia;—were indicted, convicted, condemned and shot by a little band of rebellious officers who had arrogated to themselves the function of judges. They were shot down as guilty of high treason because of a military defeat to prevent which they had put forth every possible human effort, and which they had incurred by reason of the friendliness of their English Ally, which was making use of Turkey as a convenient tool.

Frithjof Nansen in his speech of thanks for the Nobel Prize recently uttered the much reported words: "You do not know, my son, with how little reason the world is governed." It was inevitable that he should begin with the words: "As Axel Oxenstjerna once said," although I showed fully seven years ago that Oxenstjerna never said any such thing. This seems to be the only thing that intelligent men know about Oxenstjerna, and even this does not originate with Oxenstjerna.

But alas! Nansen's words are none the less true, and we have occasion every day to recognize their truth. Europe has fallen into the hands of clowns.